201 PRINCIPLES OF SOFTWARE DEVELOPMENT

Alan M. Davis
University of Colorado
at Colorado Springs

McGraw-Hill, Inc.

New York   San Francisco   Washington, D.C.   Auckland   Bogotá
Caracas   Lisbon   London   Madrid   Mexico City   Milan
Montreal   New Delhi   San Juan   Singapore
Sydney   Tokyo   Toronto

Library of Congress Cataloging-in-Publication Data

Davis, Alan M. (Alan Mark)
    201 principles of software development / Alan M. Davis.
        p.   cm.
    Includes bibliographical references and index.
    ISBN 0-07-015840-1 (acid-free paper)
    1. Computer software—Development. I. Title. II. Title: Two
hundred one principles of software development.
QA76.76.D47D377 1995
005.1—dc20   94-47075
                                                 CIP

1 2 3 4 5 6 7 8 9 0 DOC/DOC 9 0 0 9 8 7 6 5

ISBN 0-07-015840-1

The sponsoring editor for this book was Marjorie Spencer, the editing supervisor was Fred Dahl, and the production supervisor was Donald Schmidt. It was set in Palatino by Inkwell Publishing Services.

Printed and bound by R. R. Donnelley & Sons Company.

This book is printed on recycled, acid-free paper containing a minimum of 50% recycled de-inked fiber.

To order or receive additional information on these or any other
McGraw-Hill titles, in the United States please call 1-800-822-8158
In other countries, please contact your local McGraw-Hill representative.

                                                 BC15XXA

CONTENTS

Chapter 4. Design Principles   73

PREFACE

If software engineering is really an engineering discipline, it is the intelligent application of proven principles, techniques, languages, and tools to the cost-effective creation and maintenance of software that satisfies users' needs. This book is the first collection of software engineering principles ever written in one volume.* A *principle* is a basic truth, rule, or assumption about software engineering that holds regardless of the technique, tool, or language selected. With few exceptions, the principles published here are not original. They have been extracted from the writings of many software engineering practitioners and researchers. These individuals have been unselfish enough to share their experiences, ideas, and wisdom with all of us. I make no claim that these 201 principles are mutually exclusive. Unlike Boehm's seven "basic" software engineering principles, a combination of some of these principles may imply another. I also make no claim that these 201 principles are 100 percent compatible. The adages, "Absence makes the heart grow fonder" and "Out of sight, out of mind" are each true, and each can be applied to life, but they cannot both be used to justify the same decision. The principles contained in this volume are all valid, and they can all be used to improve software engineering, but it may be impossible to apply some combinations of them on any one project.

*Winston Royce and Barry Boehm published the first two papers on software engineering principles with five and seven principles, respectively [ROY70, BOE83].

Manny Lehman [LEH80] has stated eloquently why principles underlying software engineering are inherently different from principles underlying other areas of human exploration. He states there is no reason to expect such principles to have the same "precision and predictability of [say] the laws of physics." The reason for this is that, unlike physics or biology, the process of software development is "managed and implemented by people; thus in the long term [its behavior *should*] be expected to be unpredictable, dependent on the judgments, whims, and actions of [people]." On the other hand, software *does* seem to exhibit many regular and predictable traits [LEH80]. These lead to many basic principles that can be enumerated and used by inexperienced and experienced software engineers and managers to enhance the quality of both the software engineering process and software products.

The purpose of this book is to present in one volume the principles of software engineering as a reference guide. It is aimed at three classes of readers:

1. *Software engineers and managers.* In this book you can find out what is good and what is not. If you are new at software engineering or software management, here is a place to find out what you need to know.

2. *Students of software engineering.* For students, there are two primary uses of this book. First, here are the basic, nondogmatic tenets that every software engineer should know. Second, the references in these pages point to some of the best papers and books ever written on software engineering. If you do nothing other than read the items referenced, this book will have been successful, and you will have been exposed to a wealth of knowledge.

3. *Software researchers.* Researchers may often find it difficult to find the original source of an idea. I have provided references to publications that reflect either the original source or an alternative, excellent work that refers to the original source.

I sincerely hope that everybody who buys this book attempts to read as many of the referenced works as possible. My brief description of the principle is intended to be friendly, easy-to-read, and insightful. But for real appreciation you need to read the referenced works. These works are not neces-

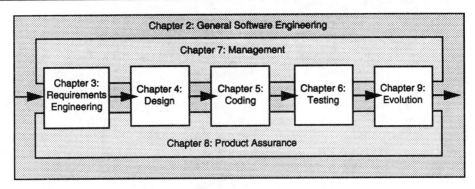

Figure P-1. *Organization of the book.*

sarily the original source of the idea (although in many cases they are). Nor is the given principle necessarily a primary point of the reference. In every case, however, the referenced work contains a wealth of helpful background, insight, justification, backup data, or information related to the principle.

In summary, this book should be the first place for you to look up any software engineering idea. However, this is a book of principles, not techniques, languages, or tools. You will not find out how to use *any* techniques, languages, or tools which the principles described here transcend. Furthermore, this book tries to avoid all fads, good or bad! For the most part, fads are popular for three to ten years, then lose favor. The underlying principles that might be behind a fad can be found in this volume, but not the fad itself. Thus, for example, you won't see any reference to object-orientation per se here, but you will find many references to the principles underlying object-orientation, such as encapsulation.

The principles are organized into general categories to aid in finding them and to aid in relating similar principles. These categories correspond to primary phases of software development (that is, requirements design, etc.) and to other critical "support" activities, such as management, product assurance, and so on, as shown in Fig. P-1.

Alan M. Davis

REFERENCES

[BOE83] Boehm, B., "Seven Basic Principles of Software Engineering," *Journal of Systems and Software, 3*, 1 (March 1983), pp. 3-24.

[LEH80] Lehman, M., "On Understanding Laws, Evolution, and Conservation in the Large-Program Life Cycle," *Journal of Systems and Software, 1*, 3 (July 1980), pp. 213-221.

[ROY70] Royce, W., "Managing the Development of Large Software Systems," *WESCON '70*, 1970; reprinted in *9th International Conference on Software Engineering*, Washington, D.C.: IEEE Computer Society Press, 1987, pp. 328-338.

ACKNOWLEDGMENTS

Stephen Andriole of Drexel University unknowingly inspired me to write this book during a class we were coteaching. I had just mentioned that software engineering, like all engineering disciplines, is driven by a set of underlying principles. My statement seemed quite logical. However, Steve challenged me: "Name one, Al. Just name one!" Luckily I think well on my feet and came up with one. He said, "Okay, name just one more, and I'll believe that there really are software engineering principles." I thought of another, and another.

Kerry Baugh was responsible for creating and maintaining the physical quality of the manuscript. Steve Andriole, Manny Lehman, and Jawed Siddiqi made contributions by reviewing early versions of the manuscript. Dr. Siddiqi was instrumental in providing advice on how to organize the principles.

Last, but not least, I want to thank my wife, Ginny, our children, Marsha and Michael, and my parents, Barney and Hannah Davis, for all their love and support and willingness to live without husband, father, or son while I spent hours writing.

201 PRINCIPLES OF SOFTWARE DEVELOPMENT

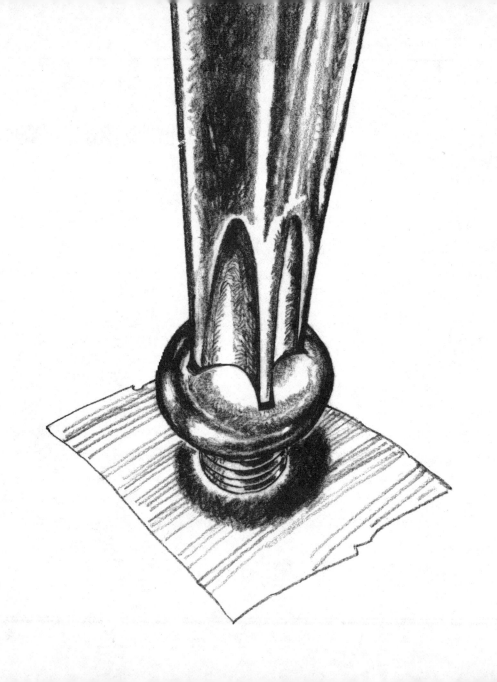

1 INTRODUCTION

This book contains a collection of principles of software engineering. These principles represent the state-of-the-art of what we believe is "right" when engineering software. Other engineering disciplines have principles based on the laws of physics, or biology, or chemistry, or mathematics. Because the product of software engineering is nonphysical, the laws of the physical do not easily form a solid foundation.

The software industry has been flooded by hundreds of books that discuss techniques, languages, and tools. None has attempted to compile the list of *underlying* principles. As shown in Fig. 1-1, *principles* are the rules to live by; they represent the collected wisdom of many dozens of people who have learned through experience. They tend to be stated as absolute truths (this is always true) or as inferences (when X occurs, Y will occur).

Techniques are step-by-step procedures that aid a software developer in performing a part of the software engineering process. Techniques tend to enforce a subset of the underlying principles. Most techniques create either documents and/or programs. Many techniques also analyze existing documents and/or programs, or they transform existing documents and/or programs into the products.

Languages consist of a set of primitive elements (such as words or graphical symbols) and a set of rules by which one can construct more complex entities (such as sentences, diagrams, models) from those primi-

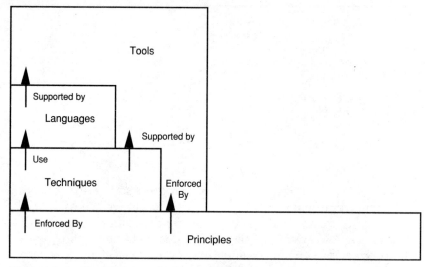

Figure 1-1. *Principles, techniques, languages, tools.*

tive elements, as well as semantics that endow each combination of entities with meaning. Languages are used to express all products of software engineering, whether intermediate or final. The documents and programs created or analyzed by techniques are typically represented in some language.

Tools are software programs that assist a software engineer in performing some step of software engineering. They may:

- Serve in an advisory capacity to the engineer (like the Knowledge-Based Requirements Assistant).
- Analyze something for conformity to a technique (a data-flow diagram checker, for example) or a subset of principles.
- Automate some aspect of software engineering (such as any compiler).
- Aid the engineer in doing some aspect of the job (as an editor).

The set of principles for a discipline evolve as the discipline grows. Existing principles are modified. New ones are added. Old ones are discarded. It is the practice and experience gained through that practice that cause us to evolve those principles. If we were to examine the set of software engineering principles from 1964 they would look downright silly today (for example, always use short variable names, or do whatever it takes to make your program smaller). Today's principles will look equally silly in thirty years.

And now, *today's* principles of software engineering.

2 GENERAL PRINCIPLES

PRINCIPLE 1
QUALITY IS #1

A customer will not tolerate a product with poor quality, regardless of the definition of quality. Quality must be quantified and mechanisms put into place to motivate and reward its achievement. It may seem politically correct to deliver a product on time, even though its quality is poor, but it is politically correct in the short term only; it is political suicide in the middle and long term. There is no trade-off to be made. The first requirement must be quality. Edward Yourdon suggests that you "Just say no" when you're asked to speed up testing, ignore a few bugs, or code before agreeing on a design or a set of requirements.

Ref: Yourdon, E., *Decline and Fall of the American Programmer*, Englewood Cliffs, N.J.: Prentice Hall, 1992 (Chapter 8).

PRINCIPLE 2
QUALITY IS IN THE EYES OF THE BEHOLDER

There is no one definition of software quality. To developers, it might be an elegant design or elegant code. To users who work in stress environments, it might be response time or high capacity. For cost-sensitive projects, it might be low development cost. For some customers, it might be satisfying all their perceived *and* not-yet-perceived needs. The dilemma is that these may not be all compatible. Optimizing one person's quality might be detrimental to another's. (This is Weinberg's "Political Dilemma" principle.) A project must decide on its priorities and articulate them to all parties.

Ref: Weinberg, G., *Quality Software Management*, Vol. 1: Systems Thinking, New York: Dorset House, 1992, Section 1.2.

PRINCIPLE 3
PRODUCTIVITY AND QUALITY ARE INSEPARABLE

There is a clear relationship between productivity (measured by numbers of widgits—whether they be lines of code or function points—per person-month) and quality. The higher the demand for quality, the lower your productivity becomes. The lower the demand for quality, the higher your productivity becomes. The more you emphasize increased productivity, the lower your resulting quality. Bell Labs has found that, to achieve one to two bugs per thousand lines of code, productivities of 150 to 300 lines of code per person-month are common [see Fleckenstein, W., "Challenges in Software Development," *IEEE Computer, 16,* 3 (March 1983), pp. 60-64]. As attempts are made to drive productivity up, the density of bugs increases.

Ref: Lehman, M., "Programming Productivity—A Life Cycle Concept," *COMPCON 81,* Washington, D.C.: IEEE Computer Society Press, 1981, Section 1.1.

PRINCIPLE 4
HIGH-QUALITY SOFTWARE IS POSSIBLE

Although our industry is saturated with examples of software systems that perform poorly, that are full of bugs, or that otherwise fail to satisfy users' needs, there are counter examples. Large-scale software systems *can* be built with very high quality, but for a steep price tag: on the order of $1000 per line of code. One such example is IBM's on-board flight software for NASA's space shuttle. Totaling approximately three million lines of code, the rigorous software development process resulted in less than one error found per ten thousand lines of code after product release.

As a developer, be aware of the techniques that have been demonstrated to increase quality considerably. These include involving the customer (Principle 8), prototyping (to verify requirements prior to full-scale development; Principles 11 through 13), keeping the design simple (Principle 67), inspections (Principle 98), and hiring the best people (Principles 130 and 131). As a customer, demand excellence but be aware of the high costs involved.

Ref: Joyce, E., "Is Error-Free Software Achievable?" *Datamation* (February 15, 1989).

PRINCIPLE 5
DON'T TRY TO RETROFIT QUALITY

Quality cannot be retrofit into software. This applies to any definition of quality: maintainability, reliability, adaptability, testability, safety, and so on. We have a very difficult time building quality into software during development when we try to. How can we possibly expect to achieve quality when we don't try? This is primarily why you must not try to convert a throwaway prototype into a product (Principle 11).

Ref: Floyd, C., "A Systematic Look at Prototyping," in *Approaches to Prototyping*, R. Budde, et al., Berlin, Germany: Springer Verlag, 1983, pp. 1-18, Section 3.1.

PRINCIPLE 6
POOR RELIABILITY IS WORSE THAN POOR EFFICIENCY

When software is not efficient, it is generally possible to isolate the sections of the program that consume most of the execution time and redesign or recode them for increased efficiency (Principle 194). Poor reliability is not only more difficult to detect, it is also more difficult to fix. A system's poor reliability may not become apparent until years after the system is deployed—and it kills somebody. Once the poor reliability manifests itself, it is often difficult to isolate its cause.

Ref: Sommerville, I., *Software Engineering*, Reading, Mass.: Addison-Wesley, 1992, Section 20.0.

PRINCIPLE 7
GIVE PRODUCTS TO CUSTOMERS EARLY

No matter how hard you try to learn users' needs during the requirements phase, the most effective means to ascertain their real needs is to give them a product and let them play with it. If you follow a conventional interpretation of the waterfall model, the first delivery of a product to the customer occurs after 99 percent of the development resources are already expended. Thus, the majority of customer feedback on their needs occurs after the resources are expended.

Contrast that with an approach, for example, of constructing a quick and dirty prototype early in the development process. Deliver this to the customer, gather feedback, and then write a requirements specification and proceed with a full-scale development. In this scenario, only 5 to 20 percent of the development resources are expended by the time customers experience their first product. If the appropriate features were built into the prototype, the highest-risk user needs will become better known and the final product is more likely to be user-satisfactory. This helps ensure that the remainder of the resources are spent building the right system.

Ref: Gomaa, H., and D. Scott, "Prototyping as a Tool in the Specification of User Requirements," *Fifth International Conference on Software Engineering*, Washington, D.C.: IEEE Computer Society Press, 1981, pp. 333-342.

PRINCIPLE 8
COMMUNICATE WITH CUSTOMERS/USERS

Never lose sight of why software is being developed: to satisfy real needs, to solve real problems. The only way to solve real needs is to communicate with those who have the needs. The customer or user is the most important person involved with your project.

If you are a commercial developer, talk often with the clients. Keep them involved. Sure, it is easier to develop software in a vacuum, but will the customer like the result? If you're a producer of shrinkwrap software, "customers" are harder to locate during development. So role-play. Designate three or four individuals in your organization as prospective customers and tap them for ideas that will keep them as customers or make them happy. If you're a government contractor, talk often with the contracting officers, their technical representatives, and, if possible, the users. People and situations change often in the government. The only way to keep up with the change is communication. Ignoring the changes may make life seem easier in the short term, but the final system will not be useful.

Ref: Farbman, D., "Myths That Miss," *Datamation* (November 1980), pp. 109-112.

PRINCIPLE 9
ALIGN INCENTIVES FOR DEVELOPER AND CUSTOMER

Projects often fail because customers and developers have different (and perhaps incompatible) goals. For example, take the simple case in which the customer wants features 1, 2, and 3 by a specific date and the developer wants to maximize revenue or profit. To maximize revenue, the developer may attempt to build all three features in their entirety even if late. Meanwhile, the customer may have preferred to be missing part of one of the features if only it could have the others on time.

To help align the two organizations' goals: (1) Prioritize requirements (Principle 50) so that developers understand their relative importance, (2) reward the developer based on the relative priorities (for example, all high-priority requirements must be satisfied, each medium priority requirement earns the developer a small additional bonus of some kind, and each low priority requirement satisfied earns a very small bonus), and (3) use strict penalties for late delivery.

PRINCIPLE 10
PLAN TO THROW ONE AWAY

One of the most important critical success factors for a project is whether it is entirely new. Programs that tread on brand new territory (whether it be with respect to application, architecture, interface, or algorithm) rarely work the first time. Fred Brooks, in his *Mythical Man Month*, makes this perfectly clear with his advice, "Plan to throw one away; you will anyway." This advice was originally presented by Winston Royce in 1970, when he said one should plan for the first fully deployed system to be the second one created. The first should at least check out the critical design issues and the operational concept. Furthermore, Royce recommended that such a prerelease version should be developed with approximately 25 percent of the total system development resources.

As a developer of a new custom product, plan to build a series of throwaway prototypes (Principles 11, 12, and 13) before embarking on the full-scale product development. As a commercial high-volume developer, expect that your first product version will be able to be modified for a certain period of years, after which it will need to be fully replaced (related Principles 185, 186, 188, and 201). As a maintainer of a product, be aware that you can fiddle with the program just so much before it becomes unstable and must be replaced (see related Principles 186, 191, 195, and 197).

Ref: Royce, W., "Managing the Development of Large Software Systems," *WESCON '70*, 1970; reprinted in *9th International Conference on Software Engineering*, Washington, D.C.: IEEE Computer Society Press, 1987, pp. 328-338.

PRINCIPLE 11
BUILD THE RIGHT KIND OF PROTOTYPE

There are two types of prototypes: throwaway and evolutionary. *Throwaway* prototypes are built in a quick and dirty manner, are given to the customer for feedback, and are thrown away once the desired information is learned. The desired information is captured in a requirements specification for a full-scale product development. *Evolutionary* prototypes are built in a quality manner, are given to the customer for feedback, and are modified once the desired information is learned to more closely approximate the needs of the users. This process is repeated until the product converges to the desired product.

Throwaway prototypes should be built when critical features are poorly understood. Evolutionary prototypes should be built when the critical functions are well understood but many other features are poorly understood. Build a throwaway prototype followed by a "from-scratch" evolutionary prototype if most functions are poorly understood.

Ref: Davis, A., "Operational Prototyping: A New Development Approach," *IEEE Software, 9,* 5 (September 1992), pp. 70-78.

PRINCIPLE 12
BUILD THE RIGHT FEATURES INTO A PROTOTYPE

When constructing a throwaway prototype, build only features that are poorly understood. After all, if you build well understood features, you will learn nothing, and you will have wasted resources. When constructing an evolutionary prototype (Principle 13), build the features that are best understood. (Note that these may have become "best understood" because they were verified previously using throwaway prototypes.) Your hope is that, by experiencing these features, users will be able to better determine additional needs. If you build a poorly understood requirement (in a quality fashion) into an evolutionary prototype, you may be wrong, you will have to discard "quality" software, and you will have wasted resources.

Ref: Davis, A., "Operational Prototyping: A New Development Approach," *IEEE Software, 9,* 5 (September 1992), pp. 70-78.

PRINCIPLE 13
BUILD THROWAWAY PROTOTYPES QUICKLY

If you've decided to build a throwaway prototype, build it as quickly as you can. Don't worry about quality. Use a one-page requirements specification. Don't worry about design or code documentation. Use any available tool. Use any language that facilitates the quick development of software applicable to your application. Do not worry about the inherent maintainability of the language.

Ref: Andriole, S., *Rapid Application Prototyping*, Wellesley, Mass.: QED, 1992.

PRINCIPLE 14
GROW SYSTEMS INCREMENTALLY

One of the most effective techniques to reduce risk in building software is to grow it incrementally. Start small, with a *working* system that implements only a few functions. Then grow it to cover larger and larger subsets of the eventual functionality. The advantages are (1) lower risk with each build, and (2) seeing a version of the product often helps users envision other functions they would like. The disadvantage is that, if an inappropriate architecture is selected early, a complete redesign may be necessary to accommodate later changes. Reduce this risk by building throwaway prototypes (Principles 11, 12, and 13) prior to starting the incremental development.

Ref: Mills, H., "Top-Down Programming in Large Systems," in *Debugging Techniques in Large Systems*, R. Ruskin, ed., Englewood Cliffs, N.J.: Prentice Hall, 1971.

PRINCIPLE 15
THE MORE SEEN, THE MORE NEEDED

It has been witnessed over and over again in the software industry: The more functionality (or performance) that is provided to a user, the more functionality (or performance) that the user will want. This, of course, supports Principles 7 (Give Products to Customers Early), 14 (Grow Incrementally), 185 (Software Will Continue to Change), and 201 (System's Existence Promotes Evolution). But more importantly, you must prepare yourself for the inevitable. Every aspect of both management and engineering processes should be aware that, as soon as the customers see the product, they will want more.

This means that every document produced should be stored and organized in a fashion conducive for change. It means configuration management procedures (Principle 174) must be in place long before delivery. It means you should be prepared for an onslaught of oral or written requests from users soon after deployment. It means that your design should be selected so that capacities, rates of inputs, and functionality can all be changed easily.

Ref: Curtis, B., H. Krasner, and N. Iscoe, "A Field Study of the Software Design Process for Large Systems," *Communications of the ACM, 31,* 11 (November 1988), pp. 1268-1287.

PRINCIPLE 16
CHANGE DURING DEVELOPMENT IS INEVITABLE

Edward Bersoff et al. define the first law of system engineering as, "No matter where you are in the system [development] life cycle, the system will change, and the desire to change it will persist throughout the life cycle." Unlike Principles 185 and 201, which emphasize that software requirements will change dramatically once deployed, this principle says software will change dramatically *during* development. These changes may reflect writing new code, new test plans, or new requirements specifications. They may mean making repairs to an intermediate product that has been found to be incorrect. Or they can reflect the natural process of perfecting or improving the product.

To prepare yourself for these changes, be sure that all products of a software development are appropriately cross-referenced to each other (Principles 43, 62, and 107), that change management procedures are in place (Principles 174 and 178 through 183), and that budgets and schedules have enough leeway so that you are not tempted to ignore necessary changes just to meet budgets and schedules (Principles 147, 148, and 160).

Ref: Bersoff, E., V. Henderson, and S. Siegel, *Software Configuration Management,* Englewood Cliffs, N.J.: Prentice Hall, 1980, Section 2.2.

PRINCIPLE 17
IF POSSIBLE, BUY INSTEAD OF BUILD

The single most effective technique to reduce escalating software development costs and risk is to buy software off the shelf instead of building it from scratch. It is true that off-the-shelf software may solve only 75 percent of your problems. But consider the alternative: Pay at least ten times as much, take the risk that the software is 100 percent over budget and late (if finished at all!), and, when it is all done, accept that it still may meet only 75 percent of your expectations.

As a consumer, new software development projects always seem exciting at first. The team is "optimistic," full of hope for the "ultimate" solution. Few software development projects run smoothly. Escalating costs usually cause requirements to be scaled back, resulting in a system that may satisfy just as many needs as an off-the-shelf system could have. As a developer, you should reuse as much software as possible. Reuse is "buying instead of building" on a less grand scale. See related Principle 84.

Ref: Brooks, F., "No Silver Bullet: Essence and Accidents of Software Engineering," *IEEE Computer, 20,* 4 (April 1987), pp. 10-19.

PRINCIPLE 18
BUILD SOFTWARE SO THAT IT NEEDS A SHORT USERS' MANUAL

One way to measure the quality of a software system is to look at the size of its users' manual. The shorter the manual, the better the software is. The use of well-designed software should be mostly self-evident. Unfortunately, too many software designers fashion themselves as experts in human interface design as well. The voluminous manuals that result are sufficient evidence that most interface designers are not as great as they proclaim themselves to be. (By the way, when I say "users' manual" I include on-line help text. Thus, software does not suddenly become better overnight by putting the users' manual on-line.)

Use standard interfaces. Use industry experts to design self-evident icons, commands, protocols, and user scenarios. And remember: Just because software developers "like" an interface, it doesn't mean that your customers will have any idea of how to use it. Many software developers like interfaces with built-in tricks that serve as short-cuts. Usually, customers want simple, clean, clear interfaces—not tricks.

Ref: Hoare, C.A.R., "Programming: Sorcery or Science?" *IEEE Software*, 1, 2 (April 1984), pp. 14-15.

PRINCIPLE 19
EVERY COMPLEX PROBLEM HAS A SOLUTION

Wlad Turski said, "To every complex problem, there is a simple solution … and it is wrong!" Be highly suspicious of anybody who offers you something like, "Just follow these 10 simple steps and your software quality problems will disappear."

Ref: Turski, W., oral comments made at a conference in the late 1970s.

PRINCIPLE 20
RECORD YOUR ASSUMPTIONS

The environments we place systems into are by their very nature infinite and impossible to fully comprehend. When we build a system, allegedly to solve a problem in that environment we make assumptions about the environment. Manny Lehman hypothesizes that "we make approximately one assumption every 10 lines of code, or even if I'm off by a factor of 2 or 3, one assumption every 20 to 30 lines of code." These finite assumptions about an infinite world can get you into trouble. Lehman describes a linear accelerator that was not behaving as expected. One physicist suggested that perhaps the phases of the moon were having an effect, to which everybody responded, "You have got to be kidding!" However, after factoring in the moon, the resulting equations accounted for a large majority of the seemingly "incorrect" behavior. This is an example of an assumption that was made (that there were no lunar effects) that was invalid.

It is impossible to be conscious of all the assumptions you make during requirements engineering, design, coding, and testing. Nonetheless, I recommend you maintain a diary of assumptions that you make consciously. Do this even if the assumption seems obvious or if the alternatives seem preposterous. Also record their implications, that is, where in the product does the assumption manifest itself? Ideally, you would like to isolate such implications by encapsulating each assumption (Principle 65).

Ref: Lehman, M., "Software Engineering, the Software Process and Their Support," *Software Engineering Journal, 6,* 5 (September 1991), pp. 243-258, Section 3.6.

PRINCIPLE 21
DIFFERENT LANGUAGES FOR DIFFERENT PHASES

The industry's eternal thirst for simple solutions to complex problems (Principle 19) drives many to declare that the best software development method would use the same notations for software representation throughout the entire development life cycle. Since this is not the case in any other engineering discipline, why should it be in software engineering? Electrical engineers use different notations for different design activities: block diagrams, circuit diagrams, logic diagrams, timing diagrams, state transition tables, stick diagrams, and so on. Notations provide us with models that can be manipulated in our minds. The more notations and the richer and more diverse the representations used, the better we can visualize the product under construction. Why would software engineers want to use, say, Ada for requirements, design, and code unless it were optimal for all? Why would they want to use, say, object-orientation for all phases unless it were optimal for all?

For requirements engineering, select a set of optimal techniques and languages (Principles 47 and 48). For design, select a set of optimal techniques and languages (Principles 63 and 81). For coding, select an optimal language (Principles 102 and 103). Transitions between phases *are* difficult. Using the same language doesn't help. On the other hand, if a language is optimal for certain aspects of two phases, by all means use it.

Ref: Matsubara, T., "Bringing up Software Designers," *American Programmer, 3,* 7 (July-August 1990), pp. 15-18.

PRINCIPLE 22
TECHNIQUE BEFORE TOOLS

An undisciplined carpenter with a power tool becomes a dangerous undisciplined carpenter. An undisciplined software engineer with a tool becomes a dangerous undisciplined software engineer. Before you use a tool, you should have discipline (that is, understand and be able to follow an appropriate software technique). Of course, you also need to know how to use the tool, but that is secondary to having good discipline.

I strongly recommend following a technique *by hand* and convincing yourself and your management that the technique works *before* investing in tools to "automate" the technique. In most cases, if a technique doesn't work without automation, it won't work with automation.

Ref: Kemerer, C., "How the Learning Curve Affects Tool Adoption," *IEEE Software, 9, 3* (May 1992), pp. 23-28.

PRINCIPLE 23
USE TOOLS, BUT BE REALISTIC

Software tools (such as CASE) make their users more efficient. By all means, use them. Just as a word processor is an essential aid to an author, a CASE tool is an essential aid to a software engineer. Each enhances its users' initial productivity by 10 to 20 percent. Each enhances its users' ability to modify and evolve their product by 25 to 50 percent, but in both cases the hard work (thinking) is not done by the tool. Use CASE but be realistic concerning its effect on productivity. Be aware that 70 percent of all CASE tools purchased are never used. I believe the primary reason for this is overoptimism and the resulting disappointment, rather than the ineffectiveness of the tools.

Ref: Kemerer, C., "How the Learning Curve Affects Tool Adoption," *IEEE Software, 9,* 3 (May 1992), pp. 23-28.

PRINCIPLE 24
GIVE SOFTWARE TOOLS TO GOOD ENGINEERS

Users of software tools (such as CASE) become more productive just as writers become more productive using word processors (Principle 23). However, just as a word processor cannot convert a poor novelist (one that writes novels that don't sell) into a good one, a CASE tool cannot convert a poor software engineer (one that produces software that is unreliable, fails to satisfy user needs, and so on) into a good one. Thus, you want to give CASE tools only to the good engineers. The last thing you want to do is to provide CASE tools to the poor engineers: You want them to produce less, not more, poor-quality software.

PRINCIPLE 25
CASE TOOLS ARE EXPENSIVE

Workstations or high-end personal computers to host a CASE environment cost between $5000 and $15,000 per seat. CASE tools themselves range from $500 to $50,000 per copy. The annual licensing and maintenance fees for tools generally cost 10 to 15 percent of their purchase price. Also, expect to pay salaries for two to three days for each employee to be trained. Thus, total expected set-up costs can exceed $17,000 per seat (for a moderately priced CASE tool) and recurring annual costs can exceed $3000 per seat.

CASE tools are essential for software development. They should be considered part of the cost of being in the business. When doing a payback analysis, take into consideration the high costs of buying the tools, but also take into account the higher costs of *not* buying the tools (lower productivity, higher probability of customer dissatisfaction, delayed product release, increased rework, poorer product quality, increased employee turnover).

Ref: Huff, C., "Elements of a Realistic CASE Tool Adoption Budget," *Communications of the ACM, 35,* 4 (April 1992), pp. 45-54.

PRINCIPLE 26
"KNOW-WHEN" IS AS IMPORTANT AS KNOW-HOW

All too often in our industry, a software engineer learns a new technique and decides that it is the be-all and end-all of techniques. Meanwhile, another software engineer on the same team learns a different new technique and an emotional battle ensues. The fact is that neither engineer is right. Knowing how to use a technique well does not make it a good technique, nor does it make you a good engineer. Knowing how to use a wood lathe well does not make you a good carpenter. The good engineer knows dozens of diverse techniques well and knows when each is appropriate for a project or a segment of a project. The good carpenter knows how to use dozens of tools, knows lots of diverse techniques, and, most importantly, knows when to employ each.

When doing requirements engineering, understand which techniques are most useful for which aspects of your problem (Principle 47). When doing design, understand which techniques are most useful for which aspects of your system (Principle 63). When coding, pick the most appropriate language (Principle 102).

PRINCIPLE 27
STOP WHEN YOU ACHIEVE YOUR GOAL

Software engineers follow many dozens of methods (also called techniques or procedures). Each of these has a purpose, usually corresponding to a subgoal of software development. For example, structured (or object-oriented) analysis has the goal of understanding the problem being solved, DARTS has the goal of a process architecture, and structured design has the goal of a calling hierarchy. In each case the method consists of a series of steps. Do not be so taken in by the method that you forget your goal. Don't be guilty of goals displacement. If, for example, you understand your problem after doing only half the steps of a method, stop. On the other hand, you need to have a good view of the entire software process because a later step of a method that appears discardable by this principle may generate something critical for later use.

PRINCIPLE 28
KNOW FORMAL METHODS

Formal methods are not easy without strong discrete mathematical skills. On the other hand, their use (even on the back of an envelope) can aid significantly in uncovering problems in many aspects of software development. At least one person on every project should be comfortable with formal methods to ensure that opportunities for building quality into the product are not lost.

Many people think that the only way to use formal methods is to specify a system completely using them. This is not true. In fact, one of the most effective methods is to write a natural language specification first. Then attempt to write parts using formal methods. Just trying to write things more formally will help you find problems in the natural language. Fix the natural language and you now have a better document. Discard the formalism if desired after it has helped you.

Ref: Hall, A., "Seven Myths of Formal Methods," *IEEE Software, 7,* 5 (September 1990), pp. 11-19.

PRINCIPLE 29
ALIGN REPUTATION WITH ORGANIZATION

It is generally recognized that Japanese software engineers view software bugs differently than American software engineers. Although many factors influence this, one relates to the perception in Japan that an error in a product is a disgrace to the company, and a disgrace to the company caused by a software engineer is a disgrace to the engineer. This works more effectively in Japan than in the United States because Japanese workers tend to remain in one company for their entire careers. The mind-set, however, is important regardless of employment longevity.

In general, when anybody finds an error in a software engineer's product, that engineer should be thankful, not defensive. To err is human. To accept, divine! When an engineering error is found, the person causing it should broadcast it, not hide it. The broadcasting has two effects: (1) It helps other engineers avoid the same error, and (2) it sets the stage for future nondefensive error repair.

Ref: Mizuno, Y., "Software Quality Improvement," *IEEE Computer, 16,* 3 (March 1983), pp. 66-72.

PRINCIPLE 30
FOLLOW THE LEMMINGS WITH CARE

If 50 million people say a foolish thing, it is still a
foolish thing.

Anatole France

Just because everybody is doing something does not make it right for you.
It *may* be right, but you need to carefully assess its applicability to your
environment. Some examples are object-orientation, software measurement (Principles 142, 143, 149, 150, and 151), software reuse (Principle 84),
process maturity (Principle 163), computer-aided software engineering
(CASE, Principles 22 through 25), and prototyping (Principles 11, 12, 13,
and 42). In all cases, these offer very positive opportunities for increased
quality, decreased cost, or increased user satisfaction. However, the advantages are available only to those organizations in which it makes sense.
Although the rewards are significant, their potentials are often oversold
and are by no means guaranteed or universal.

When you learn about a "new" technology, don't readily accept the
inevitable hype associated with it (Principle 129). Read carefully. Be realistic with respect to payoffs and risks. Run experiments before making major
commitments. But by no means can you afford to ignore "new" technolo-
gies (see related Principle 31).

Ref: Davis, A., "Software Lemmingineering," *IEEE Software, 10,* 6 (September 1993), pp.
79-81, 84.

PRINCIPLE 31
DON'T IGNORE TECHNOLOGY

Software engineering technology is evolving rapidly. You cannot afford to sit around for a few years without keeping abreast of new developments. Software engineering appears to grow by waves. Each wave brings with it a large collection of "fads" and buzzwords. Although each wave appears to last just five to seven years, the wave does not simply disappear. Instead each subsequent wave stands upon the best features of all previous waves. (Hopefully "best" means "most effective," but unfortunately it often means "most popular.")

I know of two ways to keep abreast of the technology: reading the right magazines and talking to the right people. *IEEE Software* magazine is a good place to learn about what's likely to be useful in the zero-to-five-year timeframe. *PC Week, MacWorld,* and the like are good places to learn about hardware platforms and commercially available tools and languages. To learn from talking to people, you must meet the right people. Although talking to folks in your own organization is necessary, it isn't sufficient. Try attending one or two key conferences per year. The presentations are probably not as important as the conversations you have in the hallways.

PRINCIPLE 32
USE DOCUMENTATION STANDARDS

If your project, organization, or customer demands that a documentation standard be followed, then, of course, follow it. However, never blame a standard for doing a bad job. All the standards I'm familiar with, whether government or commercial, provide organizational and content guidance.

Innovate! Follow the standard *and* do it intelligently. That means including what you know needs to be included regardless of what the standard says. It means writing in clear language. It means adding additional levels of organization that make sense. If you are not required to follow a standard, at least use one as a checklist to verify that you don't have major omissions. IEEE publishes one of the most extensive volumes of useful software documentation standards that I know.

Ref: IEEE Computer Society, *Software Engineering Standards Collection*, Washington, D.C.: IEEE Computer Society Press, 1993.

PRINCIPLE 33
EVERY DOCUMENT NEEDS A GLOSSARY

All of us become frustrated when we read a document and come across a term we do not understand. The frustration is short-lived, however, when we turn to the back and find the term defined in a glossary.

The definitions of all terms should be written in a manner that minimizes the need to look up in the glossary any of the words used in the definitions. One technique is first to explain the term in common, everyday terminology, and then add a second definition that uses other glossary terms. Terms used within definitions that are themselves defined elsewhere should be *italicized*. For example:

> **Data-flow diagram:** A graphical notation that shows the flows of information among the functions and databases of a system and parts of the environment that interface to the system. A notation used extensively in *structured analysis*, consisting of *transforms* (bubbles), *data flows* (arrows), *data stores* (two parallel lines), and *external entities* (rectangles).

PRINCIPLE 34
EVERY SOFTWARE DOCUMENT NEEDS AN INDEX

This principle is self-evident to all *readers* of software documents. It is surprising that *authors* do not realize this (considering the fact that every author wears the hat of a reader on occasion). An *index* is a list of all terms and concepts used in the document, together with one or more page numbers where the term or concept is defined, used, or referenced. This is true for requirements, design, code, test, users', and maintenance documents. The index is used when a reader wants to find information quickly, and it is essential during later maintenance or enhancement of the document.

Modern word processors facilitate index creation by providing commands to embed index references in the text. Then the word processor does the work of compiling, alphabetizing, and printing the results. Most CASE tools generate useful indexes as well.

PRINCIPLE 35
USE THE SAME NAME FOR THE SAME CONCEPT

Unlike writing fiction where maintaining the readers' interest is the number one goal, technical documentation must always use the same words to refer to the same concept and the same sentence structure for similar messages. To do otherwise would confuse the reader, causing the reader to spend time trying to determine if there was a technical message in the rewording itself. Apply this principle to all technical writing: requirements specifications, users' manuals, design documentation, in-line comments, and so on.

For example,

> THERE ARE THREE TYPES OF SPECIAL COMMANDS. REGULAR COMMANDS COME IN FOUR VARIETIES.

is not as good as:

> THERE ARE THREE TYPES OF SPECIAL COMMANDS. THERE ARE FOUR TYPES OF REGULAR COMMANDS.

Ref: Meyer, B., "On Formalism in Specifications," *IEEE Software, 2,* 1 (January 1985), pp. 6-26.

PRINCIPLE 36
RESEARCH-THEN-TRANSFER DOESN'T WORK

The literature is full of reports of incredible technical achievements in software engineering research laboratories. Few of these ever make it to software development facilities. The reasons are that:

1. In general, software researchers have little experience developing real systems.
2. Software researchers may find it easier to solve some technical problem quickly without taking the exorbitant amount of time necessary to make sure it "fits" the real world.
3. Researchers and practitioners often have such divergent vocabularies that each party finds it difficult to communicate with the other.

The result is that researchers tend to demonstrate their ideas on an ever increasing number of "toy problems."

The most successful transfers of ideas from the research laboratory to the development facility have resulted from close ties between the two facilities—from the beginning. They have used the industrial environment as the laboratory in which the ideas germinate and are demonstrated to be effective, rather than trying to do technology transfer after idea formulation.

Ref: Basili, V., and J. Musa, "The Future Engineering of Software: A Management Perspective," *IEEE Computer*, 24, 9 (September 1991), pp. 90-96.

PRINCIPLE 37
TAKE RESPONSIBILITY

In all engineering disciplines, when a design fails, the engineers are blamed. Thus, when a bridge collapses, we ask, "What did the engineers do wrong?" When software fails, the engineers are rarely blamed. If they are, the engineers respond with, "The compiler must have made a mistake," or "I was just following the 15 steps of this method," or "My manager made me do it," or "The schedule left insufficient time to do it right." The fact is that the best methods *can* be utilized in any engineering discipline to produce awful designs. And the most antiquated methods *can* be utilized in any engineering discipline to produce elegant designs.

There are no excuses. If you are the developer of a system, it is your responsibility to do it right. Take that responsibility. Do it right, or don't do it at all.

Ref: Hoare, C.A.R., "Software Engineering: A Keynote Address," *IEEE 3rd International Conference on Software Engineering*, 1978, pp. 1-4.

3 REQUIREMENTS ENGINEERING PRINCIPLES

Requirements engineering is the set of activities including (1) eliciting or learning about a problem that needs a solution, and (2) specifying the external (black box) behavior of a system that can solve that problem. The final product of requirements engineering is a requirements specification.

PRINCIPLE 38
POOR REQUIREMENTS YIELD POOR COST ESTIMATES

The top five causes for poor cost estimation all relate to the requirements process:

1. Frequent requirements changes
2. Missing requirements
3. Insufficient communication with users
4. Poor specification of requirements
5. Insufficient analysis

Use prototyping to reduce the risk of incorrect requirements. Use configuration management to control change. Plan new requirements for future releases. Use more formal approaches for requirements analysis and specification.

Ref: Lederer, A., and J. Prasad, "Nine Management Guidelines for Better Cost Estimating," *Communications of the ACM, 35,* 2 (February 1992), pp. 51-59.

PRINCIPLE 39
DETERMINE THE PROBLEM BEFORE WRITING REQUIREMENTS

When faced with what they believe is a problem, most engineers rush into offering solutions. If the engineer's perception of the problem is accurate, the solution *may* work. However, problems are often elusive. For example, Donald Gause and Gerald Weinberg describe a "problem" in a high-rise office building in which the occupants are complaining about long waits for elevators. Is this really the problem? And whose problem is it? From the occupants' perspective, the problem might be that they waste too much time. From the building owner's perspective, the problem might be that occupancy (and thus rental income) may decrease.

The obvious solution is to increase the speed of the elevators. But other ideas might include (1) adding new elevators, (2) staggering working hours, (3) reserving some elevators for express service, (4) increasing the rent (so that the owner can tolerate reduced occupancy levels), and (5) refining the "homing algorithm" used by the elevators so that they move to high-demand floors when idle. The range of costs, risks, and time delay associated with these solutions is enormous. Yet any one *could* work depending on the exact situation. Before trying to solve a problem, be sure to explore all alternative options for *who* really has the problem and *what* the problem really is. When solving the problem, don't be blinded by the potential excitement of the first solution. Procedural changes are always less expensive than system construction.

Ref: Gause, D., and G. Weinberg, *Are Your Lights On?* New York: Dorset House, 1990.

PRINCIPLE 40
DETERMINE THE REQUIREMENTS *NOW*

Requirements are hard to understand and harder to specify. The wrong solution to this problem is to do a slipshod job of requirements specification, and rush ahead to design and code in the vain hope that:

1. Any system is better than no system.
2. The requirements will work themselves out sooner or later.
3. Or the designers will figure out what can be built as they are building it.

The right solution is to do whatever it takes to learn as many of the requirements as possible *now*. Do prototyping. Talk with more customers. Work for a month with a customer to get to know his or her job firsthand. Collect data. Do whatever it takes. Now document the requirements that you understand and plan to build a system to meet those requirements. If you expect requirements to change significantly, that's okay; plan to build incrementally (Principle 14), but that is no excuse for doing a poor job of requirements specification on any one increment.

Ref: Boehm, B., "Verifying and Validating Software Requirements and Design Specifications," *IEEE Software, 1,* 1 (January 1984), pp. 75-88.

PRINCIPLE 41
FIX REQUIREMENTS SPECIFICATION ERRORS *NOW*

If you have errors in the requirements specification, they will cost you:

- Five times more to find and fix if they remain until design.
- Ten times more if they remain until coding.
- Twenty times more if they remain until unit testing.
- Two hundred times more if they remain until delivery.

That is more than convincing evidence to fix them during the requirements phase!

Ref: Boehm, B., "Software Engineering," *IEEE Transactions on Computers,* 25, 12 (December 1976), pp. 1226-1241.

PRINCIPLE 42
PROTOTYPES REDUCE RISK IN SELECTING USER INTERFACES

There is nothing as useful as a prototype for taking a low-risk, high-payoff approach for reaching agreement on a user interface prior to full-scale development. There are myriad tools to assist in creating screen displays quickly. These so-called "storyboards" give the users the impression of a real system. Not only do they help nail down requirements, they also win the hearts of the customers and users.

Ref: Andriole, S., "Storyboard Prototyping for Requirements Verification," *Large Scale Systems,* 12 (1987), pp. 231-247.

PRINCIPLE 43
RECORD WHY REQUIREMENTS WERE INCLUDED

Many activities culminate in the creation of a requirements specification: interviews, debates, discussions, architectural studies, statements of work, questionnaires, JAD/RAD sessions, requirements specifications of other systems, earlier system-level requirements. The requirements specification states the requirements that have resulted from such activities. Let us assume that a user subsequently requests a change to a requirement. We need to know the motivation for the original requirement to know whether we can safely change it. Similarly, when a system fails to satisfy a requirement, we need to know the background of the requirement before we can decide if we should modify the system to meet it or modify the requirement to match the system.

When a requirements decision is made (such as a two-second response time), record a pointer to its origin. For example, if the decision was made during an interview with a customer, record the day and time, as well as the participants in the interview. Ideally, refer explicitly to a transcript, tape recording, or video recording. It is only with such documentation that one can (1) evolve requirements later or (2) respond to situations where the as-built system fails to satisfy the requirements.

Ref: Gilb, T., *Principles of Software Engineering Management*, Reading, Mass.: Addison-Wesley, 1988, Section 9.11.

PRINCIPLE 44
IDENTIFY SUBSETS

When writing a requirements specification, clearly identify the minimal subset of requirements that might be useful. Also identify the minimal increments that might make the minimal subset more and more useful. Such identification provides software designers with insight into optimal software design. For example, it will enable designers to:

1. More easily embed just one function per component.
2. Select architectures that are more contractible and extendible.
3. And understand how to reduce functionality in the case of a schedule or budget crunch.

One very effective technique of recording subsets is to include a set of columns in the margin of the SRS beside each requirement. Each column corresponds to a different version. These versions can represent multiple flavors of a product, each tailored to a different customer or situation, or they can represent increasing levels of enhancement through time. In either case, place an "X" in the appropriate columns to indicate which versions will have which features.

Ref: Parnas, D., "Designing Software for Ease of Extension and Contraction," *IEEE Transactions on Software Engineering, 5,* 2 (March 1979), pp. 128-138.

PRINCIPLE 45
REVIEW THE REQUIREMENTS

Many parties have a stake in the success of a product development: users, customers, marketing personnel, developers, testers, quality assurance personnel, and so on. All of them also have a stake in the correctness and completeness of the requirements specification. A formal review of the SRS should be conducted prior to a major investment in the design or code.

Given that the SRS has been written in natural language, there is no easy way to review it; however, advice given by Barry Boehm on what to look for can smooth the path. Of course, if parts of the SRS have been written in more formal languages (Principles 28, 54, and 55), these parts lend themselves to manual review (due to their lack of ambiguity) and to "execution" in some cases. Executable requirements [such as Pamela Zave's PAISLey ("An Insider's Evaluation of PAISLey," *IEEE Transactions on Software Engineering, 17,* 3 (March 1991), pp. 212-225)] can be given to an appropriate tool for interpretation. With such interpretation, stakeholders can "see" how the system performs rather than just "reading" about how the system performs.

Ref: Boehm, B., "Verifying and Validating Software Requirements and Design Specifications," *IEEE Software, 1,* 1 (January 1984), pp. 75-88.

PRINCIPLE 46
AVOID DESIGN IN REQUIREMENTS

The purpose of the requirements phase is to specify *external* behavior of the solution system. This behavior should be specific enough to ensure that all designers will reach the same conclusion about intended behavior when they use the specification as an oracle. It should not, however, specify a software architecture or algorithm, for this is the realm of the designer. Designers will later select architectures and algorithms for optimal satisfaction of requirements.

If requirements writers find it difficult or impossible to specify external behavior unambiguously without looking like a design (for example, using a finite state machine to describe system behavior), then the requirements writer should include a message like this:

> WARNING: THE "DESIGN" CONTAINED HEREIN IS SUPPLIED AS AN AID IN UNDERSTANDING THE PRODUCTS' EXTERNAL BEHAVIOR ONLY. THE DESIGNERS MAY SELECT ANY DESIGN THEY WISH PROVIDED IT BEHAVES EXTERNALLY IN A MANNER IDENTICAL TO THE EXTERNAL BEHAVIOR OF THE ABOVE SYSTEM.

Ref: Davis, A., *Software Requirements: Objects, Functions and States,* Englewood Cliffs, N.J.: Prentice Hall, 1993, Section 3.1.

PRINCIPLE 47
USE THE RIGHT TECHNIQUES

No requirements technique works for all applications. The requirements for complex applications can be understood only when multiple techniques are used. Use a technique or set of techniques most appropriate for your application.

For example, use entity-relation diagrams for data-intensive applications, finite state machines or statecharts for reactive (real-time) systems, Petri nets for applications with synchrony challenges, decision tables for decision-intensive applications, and so on.

Ref: Davis A., "A Comparison of Techniques for the Specification of External System Behavior," *Communications of the ACM, 31,* 9 (September 1988), pp. 1098-1115.

PRINCIPLE 48
USE MULTIPLE VIEWS OF REQUIREMENTS

Any one "view" of requirements is insufficient to understand or describe the desired external behavior of a complex system. Instead of using structured analysis, or object-oriented analysis, or statecharts, select a combination that make sense—and use them.

For example, on a complex system, you may want to use object-oriented analysis to assess the primary real-world entities relevant to the application. OOA will help identify them and understand their interrelationships and relevant attributes. You may want to use finite-state machines to describe the desired behavior of the user interface. You may want to use decision trees to describe the desired system's behavior in response to a complex combination of external conditions, and so on.

Ref: Yeh, R., P. Zave, A. Conn, and G. Cole, Jr., "Software Requirements: New Directions and Perspectives," in *Handbook of Software Engineering*, C. Vick and C. Ramamoorthy, eds., New York: Van Nostrand Reinhold, 1984, pp. 519-543.

PRINCIPLE 49
ORGANIZE REQUIREMENTS SENSIBLY

We usually organize requirements hierarchically. This helps readers understand the system's functions and helps requirements writers locate sections when needs change. There are many ways to organize requirements; selection of the most appropriate way is dependent on the specific product.

Organize requirements in a way most natural for the customers, users, or marketing personnel. Here are some examples: by (class of) user, by (class of) stimulus, by (class of) response, by (class of) object, by (class of) feature, by system mode. Since complex systems have many requirements, use multiple organizations. For example, for a telephone switching system, organize by class of feature, then feature, then user:

1. Single-party calls
   1.1 Call forwarding
   1.2 Call park
2. Two-party calls
   2.1 Local call
      2.1.1 Calling party view
      2.1.2 Called party view

   2.2 Long distance call
      2.2.1 Calling party view
      2.2.2 Called party view
3. Multiparty calls
   3.1 Conference call
   3.2 Operator-assisted call

Ref: Davis, A., *Software Requirements: Objects, Functions, and States*, Englewood Cliffs, N.J.: Prentice Hall, 1993, Section 3.4.11.

PRINCIPLE 50
PRIORITIZE REQUIREMENTS

Not all requirements are equal. Requirements for a human-piloted space vehicle might include the presence of both instant orange juice and a functioning life support system. But clearly the former is not as important as the latter. You probably would not abort a launch if the orange juice was absent, but you would abort if the life support was not functioning.

One way to prioritize requirements is to suffix every requirement in the specification with an *M*, *D*, or *O* to connote mandatory, desirable, and optional requirements. Although this creates the oxymoronic concept of an optional requirement, it expresses clearly and precisely the relative priorities. An even better way is to rate the importance of every requirement on a scale from 0 to 10.

Ref: Davis, A., *Software Requirements: Objects, Functions, and States*, Englewood Cliffs, N.J.: Prentice Hall, 1993, Section 3.4.11.

PRINCIPLE 51
WRITE CONCISELY

I often see requirements specifications with sentences like:

> THE TARGET TRACKING FUNCTION SHALL PROVIDE THE CAPABILITY TO DISPLAY THE CURRENT TRACKING COORDINATES OF ALL ACTIVE TARGETS.

Contrast this with:

> WHEN TRACKING, THE SYSTEM SHALL DISPLAY THE CURRENT POSITIONS OF ALL ACTIVE TARGETS.

PRINCIPLE 52
SEPARATELY NUMBER EVERY REQUIREMENT

It is essential that every requirement in the requirements specification be easily referenceable. This is necessary to enable later tracing to the requirements from design (Principle 62) and from test (Principle 107).

The easiest way to do this is to tag every requirement with a unique identifier (such as "[Requirement R27]"). An alternative is to number every paragraph and then refer to a requirement in sentence k of paragraph $i.j$ as "requirement $i.j$-sk." A third alternative is to follow the rule that every requirement contains the word "shall" (or any other suitable, but reserved, word), such as, "The system shall emit a dial tone within .5 seconds of...." Then use a simple text-matching program to extract, number, and list in an appendix all requirements.

Ref: Gilb, T., *Principles of Software Engineering Management*, Reading, Mass.: Addison-Wesley, 1988, Section 8.10.

PRINCIPLE 53
REDUCE AMBIGUITY IN REQUIREMENTS

Most requirements specifications are written in natural language. Natural languages suffer from inherent ambiguity due to the imprecision of the semantics of words, phrases, and sentences. Although the only way to remove all ambiguity from the requirements is to use a formal language, it is possible to reduce ambiguity somewhat by carefully reviewing for and rewriting any sections of text with obvious or subtle ambiguity. Al Davis provides numerous examples of ambiguity and their consequences.

Three effective techniques at reducing ambiguity are:

1. Performing Fagan-type inspections on the SRS.
2. Trying to construct more formal models of the requirements and rewriting the natural language as problems are found (Principle 28).
3. Organizing the SRS so that facing pages contain natural language and more formal models, respectively.

Ref: Davis, A., *Software Requirements: Objects, Functions, and States*, Englewood Cliffs, N.J.: Prentice Hall, 1993, Section 3.4.2.

PRINCIPLE 54
AUGMENT, NEVER REPLACE, NATURAL LANGUAGE

In an effort to reduce ambiguity in requirements, software developers often decide to use a notation that is more precise than natural language. This is, of course, commendable in that ambiguity *is* reduced (Principle 53) by using finite state machines, predicate logic, Petri nets, statecharts, and the like. However, in such an effort, the specification is rendered less under-standable by others (Principle 56) who may have less computer science or mathematical background than the requirements writer.

To alleviate this problem when using a formal notation, retain the nat-ural language specification. In fact, one good idea is to keep the natural lan-guage and more formal specification side-by-side on opposing pages. Do a manual check between the two to verify conformity. The results will be that all readers can understand something and that some nonmathematical readers may learn something useful.

Ref: Meyer, B., "On Formalism in Specifications," *IEEE Software,* 2, 1 (January 1985), pp. 6-26.

PRINCIPLE 55
WRITE NATURAL LANGUAGE BEFORE A MORE FORMAL MODEL

Principle 54 says to create requirements specifications that contain both natural language and formal models. Always create the natural language first. If you write the formal model first, the tendency will be to write natural language that describes the model instead of the solution system.

Contrast these two segments to see what I mean:

> TO MAKE A LONG DISTANCE CALL, THE USER SHOULD LIFT THE PHONE. THE SYSTEM SHALL RESPOND WITH A DIAL TONE WITHIN 10 SECONDS. THE USER SHOULD DIAL A "9." THE SYSTEM SHALL RESPOND WITH A DISTINCTIVE DIAL TONE WITHIN 10 SECONDS.

> THE SYSTEM CONSISTS OF FOUR STATES: IDLE, DIAL TONE, DISTINCTIVE DIAL TONE, AND CONNECTED. TO GET FROM THE IDLE STATE TO THE DIAL TONE STATE, LIFT THE PHONE. TO GET FROM THE DIAL TONE STATE TO THE DISTINCTIVE DIAL TONE STATE, DIAL A "9."

Note that, in the latter example, the text does not help the reader at all. The best approach is to (1) write the natural language, (2) write the formal model, and (3) adapt the natural language to reduce ambiguities that become apparent when writing the formal model.

PRINCIPLE 56
KEEP THE REQUIREMENTS SPECIFICATION READABLE

A requirements specification must be read and understood by a wide range of individuals and organizations: users, customers, marketing personnel, requirements writers, designers, testers, managers, and others. The document must be written in a manner that enables all these people to fully appreciate the system needed and being built so that there are no surprises.

Creation of multiple requirements specifications (each for a subset of the stakeholders) works only if you can guarantee consistency across the versions. A more effective method is to maintain the natural language (Principle 54) while incorporating multiple views of a more formal nature (Principles 48 and 53).

Ref: Davis, A., *Software Requirements: Objects, Functions, and States*, Englewood Cliffs, N.J.: Prentice Hall, 1993, Section 3.4.6.

PRINCIPLE 57
SPECIFY RELIABILITY SPECIFICALLY

Software reliability is difficult to specify. Don't make the problem even more difficult by being vague. For example, "THE SYSTEM SHALL BE 99.999 PERCENT RELIABLE" means nothing. Does it mean that the system cannot be "down" more often than 5 minutes every year but that it is okay to occasionally make a mistake (for example, a telephone system may occasionally misdirect a phone call). Or does it mean that it must make no more than one mistake every 100,000 transactions (for instance, a patient monitoring system cannot "kill" more than one out of every 100,000 patients)?

When writing reliability requirements, differentiate between:

1. *Failure on demand.* What is the likelihood, measured as a percentage of requests, that the system will fail to respond correctly? For example, "THE SYSTEM SHALL CORRECTLY REPORT 99.999 PERCENT OF PATIENT VITAL SIGN ANOMALIES."

2. *Rate of failure.* This is the same as "failure on demand" but it is measured as a percentage of time. For example, "THE SYSTEM MAY FAIL TO REPORT A PATIENT VITAL SIGN ANOMALY NO MORE OFTEN THAN ONCE PER YEAR."

3. *Availability.* What percentage of time may the system be unavailable for use? For example, "THE TELEPHONE SYSTEM SHALL BE AVAILABLE 99.999 PERCENT OF THE TIME IN ANY GIVEN CALENDAR YEAR."

Ref: Sommerville, I., *Software Engineering*, Reading, Mass.: Addison-Wesley, 1992, Section 20.1.

PRINCIPLE 58
SPECIFY WHEN ENVIRONMENT VIOLATES "ACCEPTABLE" BEHAVIOR

Requirements specifications often define characteristics of the system's environment. This information is used in making intelligent design decisions. It also often implies that the developer is contractually obligated to accommodate such characteristics. What happens after deployment when the environment exceeds the specified limits?

Suppose the requirements for an air traffic controller system specify that the system shall handle up to 100 aircraft in a sector simultaneously. The system is built and correctly satisfies this requirement. Three years later 101 aircraft accidentally enter a sector. What should the software do? The possibilities are:

1. Print an error message, "Environment is violating the requirements."
2. Crash (the software stops).
3. Ignore the 101st aircraft.
4. Process all 101 aircraft but perhaps not satisfy some other timing constraint (such as how often the screen is updated).

Obviously, options 1, 2, and 3 are unacceptable. Yet they are valid system responses as (not) stated in the requirements. The right solution is to explicitly state in the SRS the expected system response when the environment exceeds any of the constraints defined for it.

Ref: Davis, A., *Software Requirements: Objects, Functions and States*, Englewood Cliffs, N.J.: Prentice Hall, 1993, Section 5.3.2.

PRINCIPLE 59
SELF-DESTRUCT TBD'S

It is often preached that a requirements specification should contain no TBDs (To Be Determined). Obviously, a specification with a TBD is not complete, but there may be very good reasons for approving and perhaps baselining the document with the TBD. This is particularly true for requirements whose precision are not critical to fundamental design decisions.

When you create a TBD, be sure to footnote it with a "self-destruction note," that is, specify *who* will resolve the TBD and by *when*. For example, such a footnote might say, "The software development manager will replace this TBD no later than December 1995." This assures that the TBD does not remain forever.

Ref: IEEE, *ANSI/IEEE Guide to Software Requirements Specifications,* Standard 830-1994, Washington, D.C.: IEEE Computer Society Press, 1994.

PRINCIPLE 60
STORE REQUIREMENTS IN A DATABASE

Requirements are complex and highly volatile. For these reasons, storing them in electronic media, preferably a database, is a good idea. This will facilitate making changes, finding implications of changes, recording attributes of specific requirements, and so on.

Some of the things you want to store in the database are unique identifier (Principle 52), the text of the requirement, its relationship to other requirements (such as more abstract or more detailed descriptions of the requirement), importance (Principle 50), expected volatility, pointers to its sources (Principle 43), applicable product versions (Principles 44 and 178), and so on. Ideally, the requirements specification itself is nothing but an organized "dump" of the entire database.

4 DESIGN PRINCIPLES

Design is the set of activities including (1) defining an architecture for the software that satisfies the requirements and (2) specifying an algorithm for each software component in the architecture. The architecture includes a specification of all the building blocks of the software, how they interface with each other, how they are composed of one another, and how copies of components are instantiated (that is, copies made in memory of components and executed) and destroyed. The final product of design is a design specification.

PRINCIPLE 61
TRANSITION FROM REQUIREMENTS TO DESIGN IS NOT EASY

Requirements engineering culminates in a requirements specification, a detailed description of the *external* behavior of a system. The first step of design synthesizes an optimal software architecture. There is no reason why the transition from requirements to design should be any easier in software engineering than in any other engineering discipline. Design *is* hard. Converting from an external view to an internal optimal design is fundamentally a difficult problem.

Some methods claim transition is easy by suggesting that we use the "architecture" of the requirements specification as *the* architecture. Since design *is* difficult there are three possibilities:

1. No thought went into selecting an optimal design during requirements. In this case, you cannot afford to accept the design as *the* design.
2. Alternative designs were enumerated and analyzed and best selected, all during requirements. Organizations cannot afford the effort to do a thorough design (typically 30 to 40 percent of total development costs) prior to baselining requirements, making a make/buy decision, and making a development cost estimate.
3. The method assumes that some architecture is optimal for all applications. This is clearly not possible.

Ref: Cherry, G., *Software Construction by Object-Oriented Pictures*, Canadaigua, New York: Thought Tools, 1990, p. 39.

PRINCIPLE 62
TRACE DESIGN TO REQUIREMENTS

When designing software, the designer must know which requirements are being satisfied by each component. When selecting a software architecture, it is important that all requirements are "covered." After deployment, when a failure is detected, maintainers need to quickly isolate the software components most likely to contain the cause of the failure. During maintenance, when a software component is repaired, maintainers need to know what other requirements might be adversely affected.

All these needs can be satisfied by the creation of a large binary table with rows corresponding to all software components and columns corresponding to every requirement in the SRS. A 1 in any position indicates that this design component helps to satisfy this requirement. Notice that a *row* void of 1's indicates that a component has no purpose and a *column* void of 1's indicates an unfulfilled requirement. Some people argue that this table is very difficult to maintain. I would argue that you *need* this table to design or maintain software. Without the table, you are likely to design a software component incorrectly, spending exorbitant amounts of time during maintenance. The successful creation of such a table depends on your ability to refer uniquely to every requirement (Principle 52).

Ref: Glass, R., *Building Quality Software*, Englewood Cliffs, N.J.: Prentice Hall, 1992, Section 2.2.2.5.

PRINCIPLE 63
EVALUATE ALTERNATIVES

A critical aspect of all engineering disciplines is the elaboration of multiple approaches, trade-off analyses among them, and the eventual adoption of one. After requirements are agreed upon, you *must* examine a variety of architectures and algorithms. You certainly do not want to use an architecture simply because it was used in the requirements specification (Principle 46). After all, that architecture was selected to optimize understandability of the system's external behavior. The architecture you want is the one that optimizes conformance with the requirements contained in the requirements specification.

For example, architectures are generally selected to optimize throughput, response time, modifiability, portability, interoperability, safety, or availability, while also satisfying the functional requirements. The best way to do this is to enumerate a variety of software architectures, analyze (or simulate) each with respect to the goals, and select the best alternative. Some design methods result in specific architectures; so one way to generate a variety of architectures is to use a variety of methods.

Ref: Weinberg, G., *Rethinking Systems Analysis and Design*, New York: Dorset House, 1988, Part V.

PRINCIPLE 64
DESIGN WITHOUT DOCUMENTATION IS *NOT* DESIGN

I have often heard software engineers say, "I have finished the design. All that's left is its documentation." This makes no sense. Can you imagine a building architect saying, "I have completed the design of your new home. All that's left is to draw a picture of it," or a novelist saying "I have completed the novel. All that's left is to write it"? Design *is* the selection, abstraction, and recording of an appropriate architecture and algorithm onto paper or other medium.

Ref: Royce, W., "Managing the Development of Large Software Systems," *WESCON '70*, 1970; reprinted in *9th International Conference on Software Engineering*, Washington, D.C.: IEEE Computer Society Press, 1987, pp. 328-338.

PRINCIPLE 65
ENCAPSULATE

Information hiding is a simple, proven concept that results in software that is easier to test and easier still to maintain. Most software modules should hide some information from all other software. This information could be the structure of data, the contents of data, an algorithm, a design decision, or an interface to hardware, to a user, or to another piece of software. Information hiding aids in isolating faults because, when the hidden information becomes unacceptable in some manner (such as when it fails or it must be changed to accommodate a new requirement), only the piece of software hiding that information need be examined or altered. *Encapsulation* refers to a uniform set of rules about which types of information should be hidden. For example, encapsulation in object-oriented design usually refers to the hiding of attributes (data) *and* methods (algorithms) inside each object. No other objects may effect the values of the attributes except via requests to the methods.

Ref: Parnas, D., "On the Criteria to Be Used in Decomposing Systems into Modules," *Communications of the ACM, 15,* 12 (December 1972), pp. 1053-1058.

PRINCIPLE 66
DON'T REINVENT THE WHEEL

When electrical engineers design new printed circuit boards, they go to a catalog of available integrated circuits to select the most appropriate components. When electrical engineers design new integrated circuits, they go to a catalog of standard cells. When architects design new homes, they go to catalogs of prefabricated doors, windows, moldings, and other components. All this is called "engineering." Software engineers usually reinvent components over and over again; they rarely salvage existing software components. It is interesting that the software industry calls this rare practice "reuse" rather than "engineering."

Ref: Ramamoorthy, C. V., V. Garg, and A. Prakash, "Programming in the Large," *IEEE Transactions on Software Engineering, 12,* 7 (July 1986), pp. 769-783.

PRINCIPLE 67
KEEP IT SIMPLE

A simple architecture or a simple algorithm goes a long way toward achieving high maintainability. Remember KISS. Also, as you decompose software into subcomponents, remember that a human has difficulty comprehending more than seven (plus or minus two) things at once. C. A. R. Hoare has said:

> There are two ways of constructing a software design. One way is to make it so simple that there are obviously no deficiencies and the other is to make it so complicated that there are no obvious deficiencies.

Ref: Miller, G., "The Magical Number Seven, Plus or Minus Two," *The Psychological Review, 63,* 2 (March 1956), pp. 81-97.

PRINCIPLE 68
AVOID NUMEROUS SPECIAL CASES

As you design your algorithms, you will undoubtedly realize that there are exceptional situations. Exceptional situations cause special cases to be added to your algorithm. Every special case makes it more difficult for you to debug and for others to modify, maintain, and enhance.

If you find too many special cases, you probably have an inappropriate algorithm. Rethink and redesign the algorithm. See related Principle 67.

Ref: Zerouni, C., as reported by Bentley, J., *More Programming Pearls*, Reading, Mass.: Addison-Wesley, 1988, Section 6.1.

PRINCIPLE 69
MINIMIZE INTELLECTUAL DISTANCE

Edsger Dijkstra defined *intellectual distance* as the distance between the real-world problem and the computerized solution to that problem. Richard Fairley argues that the smaller the intellectual distance, the easier it will be to maintain the software.

To do this, the structure of the software should as closely as possible mimic the structure of the real world. Design approaches such as object-oriented design and Jackson System Development have minimal intellectual distance as primary design drivers. But you can minimize intellectual distance using *any* design approach. Be aware, of course, that the "structure of the real world" is not unique. As pointed out so well by Jawed Siddiqi in his March 1994 article in *IEEE Software,* entitled "Challenging Universal Truths of Requirements Engineering," different humans often perceive different structures when examining the same real world and thus construct quite diverse "constructed realities."

Ref: Fairley, R., *Software Engineering Concepts,* New York: McGraw-Hill, 1985.

PRINCIPLE 70
KEEP DESIGN UNDER INTELLECTUAL CONTROL

A design is under intellectual control if it has been created and documented in a manner that enables its creators and maintainers to fully understand it.

An essential attribute of such a design is that it is constructed hierarchically and with multiple views. Hierarchies enable readers to comprehend the entire system abstractly, and then comprehend finer and finer levels of details as they move down the hierarchy. At each level the component should be described from an external point of view only (Principle 80). Furthermore, any single component (at any level in the hierarchy) should exhibit simplicity and elegance.

Ref: Witt, B., F. Baker, and E. Merritt, *Software Architecture and Design*, New York: Van Nostrand Reinhold, 1994, Section 2.5.

PRINCIPLE 71
MAINTAIN CONCEPTUAL INTEGRITY

Conceptual integrity is an attribute of a quality design. It implies that a limited number of design "forms" are used and that they are used uniformly. Design forms include the way components inform their callers of error conditions, how the software informs users of error conditions, how data structures are organized, mechanisms for component communication, documentation standards, and so on.

When a design is complete, it should look as if one person created it all, even though it is the product of many devoted people. During the design process, there are often temptations to diverge from the accepted forms. It is okay to give in to such temptations if the justification is for additional integrity, elegance, simplicity, or performance of the system. It is not okay to give in solely to ensure that designer x has left his or her mark on the design. Ego satisfaction is not as important as conceptual integrity.

Ref: Witt, B., F. Baker, and E. Merritt, *Software Architecture and Design,* New York: Van Nostrand Reinhold, 1994, Section 2.6.

PRINCIPLE 72
CONCEPTUAL ERRORS ARE MORE SIGNIFICANT THAN SYNTACTIC ERRORS

When creating software, whether writing requirements specifications, design specifications, code, or tests, we spend considerable effort to remove syntactic errors. This is laudable. However, the real difficulty in constructing software arises from conceptual errors. Most developers spend more time looking for and correcting syntactic errors because, when found, these look like silly errors that in some way amuse the developer. In contrast to these, developers often feel in some way flawed, or incompetent, when they locate a conceptual error. No matter how good you are, you will make conceptual errors. Look for them.

Ask yourself key questions at each phase of development. During requirements ask yourself, "Is this what the customer wants?" During design, "Will this architecture behave appropriately under stress conditions?" or "Does this algorithm really work in all situations?" During coding, "Does this code do what I think it does?" or "Does this code correctly implement the algorithm?" During test, "Does the execution of this text convince me of anything?"

Ref: Brooks, F., "No Silver Bullet: Essence and Accidents of Software Engineering," *IEEE Computer, 20,* 4 (April 1987), pp. 10-19.

PRINCIPLE 73
USE COUPLING AND COHESION

Coupling and cohesion were defined in the 1970s by Larry Constantine and Edward Yourdon. They are still the best ways we know of measuring the inherent maintainability and adaptability of a software system. In short, *coupling* is a measure of how interrelated two software components are. *Cohesion* is a measure of how related the functions performed by a software component are. We want to strive for low coupling and high cohesion. *High coupling* implies that, when we change a component, changes to other components are likely. *Low cohesion* implies difficulty in isolating the causes of errors or places to adapt to meet new requirements. Constantine and Yourdon even provided us with a simple-to-use way to measure the two concepts. Most books on software design since 1979 describe these measures. Learn them. Use them to guide your design decisions.

Ref: Constantine, L., and E. Yourdon, *Structured Design*, Englewood Cliffs, N.J.: Prentice Hall, 1979.

PRINCIPLE 74
DESIGN FOR CHANGE

During software development, we regularly uncover errors, new requirements, or the results of earlier miscommunication. All these cause the design to change even before it is baselined (see related Principle 16). Furthermore, after baselining the design and delivering the product, even more new requirements will appear (see related Principle 185). All this means that you must select architectures, components, and specification techniques to accommodate major and incessant change.

To accommodate change, the design should be:

- *Modular,* that is, it should be composed of independent parts that can be easily upgraded or replaced with a minimum of impact on other parts (see related Principles 65, 70, 73, and 80).
- *Portable,* that is, it should be easily altered to accommodate new host machines and operating systems.
- *Malleable,* that is, flexible to accommodate new requirements that had not been anticipated.
- *Of minimal intellectual distance* (Principle 69).
- *Under intellectual control* (Principle 70).
- Such that it exhibits *conceptual integrity* (Principle 71).

Ref: Witt, B., F. Baker, and E. Merritt, *Software Architecture and Design,* New York: Van Nostrand Reinhold, 1994, Section 1.3.

PRINCIPLE 75
DESIGN FOR MAINTENANCE

The largest postdesign cost risk for nonsoftware products is manufacturing. The largest postdesign cost risk for software products is maintenance. In the former case, design for manufacturability is a major design driver. Unfortunately, design for maintainability is not the standard for software. It should be.

A designer has the responsibility to select an optimal software architecture to satisfy the requirements. Obviously, the appropriateness of this architecture will have a profound effect on system performance. However, the selection of this architecture also has a profound effect on the maintainability of the final product. Specifically, architecture selection is more significant than algorithms or code as far as its effect on maintainability.

Ref: Romach, H. D., "Design Measurement: Some Lessons Learned," *IEEE Software*, 7, 2 (March 1990), pp. 17-25.

PRINCIPLE 76
DESIGN FOR ERRORS

No matter how much you work on your software, it *will* have errors. You should make design decisions to optimize the likelihood that:

1. Errors are not introduced.
2. Errors that are introduced are easily detected.
3. Errors that remain in the software after deployment are either noncritical or are compensated for during execution so that the error does not cause a disaster.

Such robustness is not easy to incorporate into a design. Some of the ideas that help include the following:

1. Never "fall out of a case statement." For example, if there are four possible values for a variable, don't check just for three and assume that the fourth is the only remaining possibility. Instead, assume the impossible; check for the fourth value and trap the error condition early.
2. Predict as many "impossible" conditions that you can and develop strategies for recovery.
3. To eliminate conditions that may cause disasters, do fault tree analysis for predictable unsafe conditions [see Leveson, N., "Software Safety: What, Why, and How," ACM *Computing Surveys*, *18*, 2 (June 1986), pp. 125-163].

Ref: Witt, B., F. Baker, and E. Merritt, *Software Architecture and Design*, New York: Van Nostrand Reinhold, 1994, Section 6.4.2.6.

PRINCIPLE 77
BUILD GENERALITY INTO SOFTWARE

A software component exhibits *generality* if it can perform its intended functions without any change in a variety of situations. General software components are more difficult to design than less general components. They also usually run slower when executing. However, such components:

1. Are ideal in complex systems where a similar function must be performed in a variety of places.
2. Are more potentially reusable in other systems with no modification.
3. Reduce maintenance costs for an organization due to reduced numbers of unique or similar components.

When decomposing a system into its subcomponents, stay cognizant of the potential for generality. Obviously, when a similar function is needed in multiple places, construct just one general function rather than multiple similar functions. Also, when constructing a function needed in just one place, build in generality where it makes sense—for future enhancements.

Ref: Parnas, D., "Designing Software for Ease of Extension and Contraction," *IEEE Transactions on Software Engineering, 5*, 2 (March 1979), pp. 128-138.

PRINCIPLE 78
BUILD FLEXIBILITY INTO SOFTWARE

A software component exhibits *flexibility* if it can be easily modified to perform its function (or a similar function) in a different situation. Flexible software components are more difficult to design than less flexible components. However, such components (1) are more run-time-efficient than general components (Principle 77) and (2) are more easily reused than less flexible components in diverse applications.

Ref: Parnas, D., "Designing Software for Ease of Extension and Contraction," *IEEE Transactions on Software Engineering,* 5, 2 (March 1979), pp. 128-138.

PRINCIPLE 79
USE EFFICIENT ALGORITHMS

Knowledge of the theory of algorithm complexity is an absolute prerequisite for being a good designer. Given any specific problem, you could specify an infinite number of alternative algorithms to solve it. The theory of "analysis of algorithms" provides us with the knowledge of how to differentiate between algorithms that will be inherently slow (regardless of how well they are coded) and those that will be orders of magnitude faster. Dozens of excellent books exist on this subject. Every good undergraduate computer science program will offer a course on it.

Ref: Horowitz, E., and S. Sahni, *Fundamentals of Computer Algorithms*, Potomac, Md.: Computer Science Press, 1978.

PRINCIPLE 80
MODULE SPECIFICATIONS PROVIDE ALL THE INFORMATION THE USER NEEDS AND NOTHING MORE

A key part of the design process is the precise definition of each and every software component in the system. This specification will become the "visible" or "public" part of the component. It must include everything a user* needs, such as its purpose, its name, its method of invocation, and details of how it communicates with its environment. Anything that the user does not need should be specifically excluded. In most cases, the algorithms and internal data structures used should be excluded. For if these were "visible," users might utilize this information. Subsequent enhancement or modification then becomes profoundly more difficult because any change to the component has a cascading effect on all components that use it. See related Principle 65 on encapsulation.

Ref: Parnas, D., "A Technique for Software Module Specification with Examples," *Communications of the ACM, 15,* 5 (May 1972), pp. 330-336.

*In this case, a "user" means another software component or a programmer of another component.

PRINCIPLE 81
DESIGN IS MULTIDIMENSIONAL

When designing a home, architects represent it in many ways to fully understand and convey its essence to builders, buyers of materials, and home buyers: elevations, floor plans, framing, trusses, electrical routing, plumbing routing, concrete shape, door and window framing details, and other points of view. The same is true for software design.

A complete software design includes at least:

1. *Packaging.* Often drawn as a hierarchy chart, this captures "what is part of what?" It often implies data visibility. It also shows encapsulation, such as data and functions within objects.
2. *Needs hierarchy.* This captures "who needs whom?" Drawn as a network of components, arrows indicate which components need something. The needs might be data, logic, or any other information.
3. *Invocation.* This captures "who invokes whom?" Drawn as a network of components, arrows indicate which components "call," "interrupt," or "send messages to" others.
4. *Processes.* Sets of components are packaged together as asynchronous processes. These are copies of components that are running simultaneously with other processes. Zero, one, or more copies may exist at one time. This should also specify conditions that cause a process to be created, executed, stopped, and destroyed.

Ref: Witt, B., F. Baker, and E. Merritt, *Software Architecture and Design*, New York: Van Nostrand Reinhold, 1994, Section 1.1.

PRINCIPLE 82
GREAT DESIGNS COME FROM GREAT DESIGNERS

The difference between a poor design and a good design may be the result of a sound design method, superior training, better education, or other factors. However, a really great design is the brainchild of a really great designer. Great designs are clean, simple, elegant, fast, maintainable, and easy to implement. They are the result of inspiration and insight, not just hard work or following a step-by-step design method. Invest heavily in your best designers. They are your future.

Ref: Brooks, F., "No Silver Bullet: Essence and Accidents of Software Engineering," *IEEE Computer, 20,* 4 (April 1987), pp. 10-19.

PRINCIPLE 83
KNOW YOUR APPLICATION

No matter how well the requirements have been written, the selection of optimal architectures and algorithms is very much a function of knowing the unique characteristics of an application. Expected behavior under stress situations, expected frequency of inputs, life-critical nature of response times, likelihood of new hardware, impact of weather on expected system performance, and so on are all application-specific and often demand a specific subset of possible alternative architectures and algorithms.

Ref: Curtis, B., H. Krasner, and N. Iscoe, "A Field Study of the Software Design Process for Large Systems," *Communications of the ACM, 31,* 11 (November 1988), pp. 1268-1287.

PRINCIPLE 84
YOU *CAN* REUSE WITHOUT A BIG INVESTMENT

Chances are that the most effective way to reuse software components is from a repository of crafted, hand-picked items that were tailored specifically for reuse. However, this requires considerable investment in both time and money. It is possible to reuse in the short term through a technique called salvaging. Simply stated, *salvaging* is asking others in the organization, "Have you ever built a software component that does *x*?" You find it, you adapt it, you employ it. This may not be efficient in the long term, but it certainly works now; and then you have no more excuses not to reuse.

Ref: Incorvaia, A. J., A. Davis, and R. Fairley, "Case Studies in Software Reuse," *Fourteenth IEEE International Conference on Computer Software and Applications,* Washington, D.C.: IEEE Computer Society Press, 1990, pp. 301-306.

PRINCIPLE 85
"GARBAGE IN, GARBAGE OUT" IS INCORRECT

Many people quote the expression "garbage in, garbage out" as if it were acceptable for software to behave like this. It isn't. If a user provides invalid input data, the program should respond with an intelligent message that describes why the input was invalid. If a software component receives invalid data, it should not process it, but instead should return an error code back to the component that transmitted the invalid data. This mindset helps diminish the domino effect caused by software faults and makes it easier to determine error causes by (1) catching the fault early and (2) preventing subsequent data corruption.

Ref: McConnell, S., *Code Complete*, Redmond, Wash.: Microsoft Press, 1993, Section 5.6.

PRINCIPLE 86
SOFTWARE RELIABILITY *CAN* BE ACHIEVED THROUGH REDUNDANCY

In hardware systems, high reliability or availability (Principle 57) is often achieved through redundancy. Thus, if a system component is expected to exhibit a mean-time-between-failures of x, we can manufacture two or three such components and run them in either:

1. *Parallel.* For example, they all do all the work and, when their responses differ, one is turned off with no impact on overall system functionality.
2. Or *cold standby*. A backup computer might be powered on only when a hardware failure is detected in the operational computer.

Manufacturing cost is slightly more than doubled. Design cost increases slightly. Reliability increases exponentially.

In software systems, we cannot use the same approach. If we make two copies of the same software, no increase in reliability will be achieved. If one fails, the other will as well. What *can* be done, however, is to design (using two different design teams) two versions of the software from the same requirements specification, and deploy them in parallel. Development cost doubles. Reliability increases exponentially. Notice that, in the case of hardware, design increases in cost only slightly, whereas software design cost (the primary cost of software) doubles. Ultrahigh reliability in software *is* very expensive. (Principle 4.)

Ref: Musa, J., A. Iannino, and K. Okumoto, *Software Reliability*, New York: McGraw-Hill, 1987, Section 4.2.2.

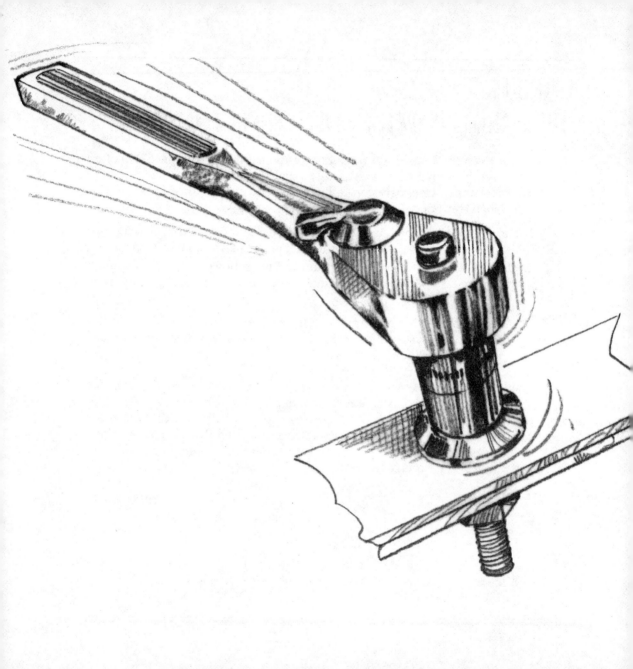

5 CODING PRINCIPLES

Coding is the set of activities including:

1. Translating the algorithms specified during design into programs written in a computer language.
2. Translating, usually automatically, the programs into a language directly executable by a computer.

The primary output of coding is a documented program listing.

PRINCIPLE 87
AVOID TRICKS

Many programmers love to create programs with *tricks*. These are constructs that perform a function correctly, but in a particularly obscure manner. Typically, they use a side-effect of a function to implement a primary function. Programmers see these as "clever," but, as Allen Macro points out, they "are often merely the stupid use of high intelligence."

There are many ways to explain why tricks are used so often:

1. Programmers are extremely intelligent and want to demonstrate that intelligence.
2. Maintainers, when they finally figure out how the trick works, will not only recognize how smart the original programmer was, but also will realize how smart they themselves are.
3. Job security.

Bottom line: Show the world how smart you are by avoiding tricky code!

Ref: Macro, A., *Software Engineering: Concepts and Management,* Englewood Cliffs, N.J.: Prentice-Hall International, 1990, p. 247.

PRINCIPLE 88
AVOID GLOBAL VARIABLES

Global variables make it convenient to write programs; after all, if you need to access or change x, you just do it. Unfortunately, if x is ever accessed and found to have an inappropriate value (say, -16.3 ships), it is difficult to determine which software component is at fault. "Global" implies that anybody could have altered its value incorrectly.

As an alternative, encapsulate important data in its own module (Principle 65), so that anybody who wants to change it or access it must do so by means of that routine. Alternatively, explicitly pass parameters to routines that need specific data. If you find an excessive number of parameters, perhaps your design needs to be reworked.

Ref: Ledgard, H., *Programming Practice,* Vol. II, Reading, Mass.: Addison-Wesley, 1987, Chap. 4.

PRINCIPLE 89
WRITE TO READ TOP-DOWN

People generally read a program from top (i.e., first line) to bottom (i.e., last line). Write a program to help the reader understand it.

Among the implications of this principle are:

1. Include a detailed external specification up front to clearly define the program purpose and use.
2. Specify externally accessed routines, local variables, and algorithms up front.
3. Use the so-called "structured" programming constructs, which are inherently easier to follow.

Ref: Kernighan, B., and P. Plauger, *The Elements of Programming Style*, New York: McGraw-Hill, 1978, pp. 20-37.

PRINCIPLE 90
AVOID SIDE-EFFECTS

A *side-effect* of a procedure is something the procedure does that is not its main purpose and that is visible (or whose results are perceivable) from outside the procedure. Side-effects are the sources of many subtle errors in software, that is, the ones that are the most latent and the ones that are most difficult to discover once their symptoms manifest themselves.

Ref: Ledgard, H., *Programming Proverbs*, Rochelle Park, N.J.: Hayden Book Company, 1975, Proverb 8.

PRINCIPLE 91
USE MEANINGFUL NAMES

Some programmers insist on naming variables with names like N_FLT, or worse, like F. The usual argument is that it makes programmers more productive because of reduced key presses. Good programmers should spend a very small percentage of their time typing (maybe 10 to 15 percent); most time should be spent thinking. So how much time is really being saved? But an even better argument is that overly shortened names actually *decrease* productivity. There are two reasons: (1) Testing and maintenance costs rise because people spend time trying to decode names, and (2) *more* time could be spent typing when using shortened names! The second argument is true because of the necessity to add comments. For example,

    N_FLT = N_FLT+1

needs a comment "LOOK AT NEXT FLIGHT" (32 keypresses), but

    NEXT_FLIGHT = PREVIOUS_FLIGHT+1

needs no such comment (29 keypresses).

Ref: Ledgard, H., *Programming Proverbs*, Rochelle Park, N.J.: Hayden Book Company, 1975, pp. 94-98.

PRINCIPLE 92
WRITE PROGRAMS FOR PEOPLE FIRST

In the early days of computing, computers were relatively slow. Almost anything that could be done to shave off a few instructions was worth the effort. The most efficient use of any of the resources on the very expensive computer system was the major goal. Things have changed. The most valuable resource is now labor: labor to develop the software, labor to maintain the software, and labor to enhance capability. With few application exceptions, programmers should think first of the people who will later attempt to understand and adapt the software. Anything that can be done to assist them should be done (Principles 87 through 91 offer some help). Efficiency is also important (Principles 63, 79, and 94), but they are not mutually exclusive. If you need efficiency, that's fine, but *upgrade* the readability of your program so that you don't lose the humans in the process.

Ref: McConnell, S., *Code Complete*, Redmond, Wash.: Microsoft Press, 1993, Section 32.3.

PRINCIPLE 93
USE OPTIMAL DATA STRUCTURES

The structure of data and the structure of programs manipulating that data are intimately interrelated. If you select the right data structures, your algorithms (and thus your code) become easy to write, and easy to read, and therefore easy to maintain. Read any book on algorithms or on data structures (they're one and the same!).

When preparing to write a program, you should develop the algorithms and data structures together. Try two or three or more different pairs before you select the best one. And be sure to encapsulate the data structure in *one* component (Principle 65) so that, when you later find a better structure, you can change it easily.

Ref: Kernighan, B., and P. Plauger, *The Elements of Programming Style*, New York: McGraw-Hill, 1988, pp. 52, 67.

PRINCIPLE 94
GET IT RIGHT BEFORE YOU MAKE IT FASTER

It is far easier to adapt a working program to make it run faster than to adapt a fast program to make it work. Don't worry about optimization when doing your initial coding. [On the other hand, don't use a ridiculously inefficient algorithm or set of data structures (Principles 79 and 93).]

Every software project has tough schedule pressures. Some may not be very pressured during their early phases, but even they step up the pace later. Given this situation, anytime a component is produced on (or ahead of) time and it works reliably, it is cause for celebration. Try to be the reason for celebration rather than desperation. If you get your program working (however slowly it runs), everybody on your team will appreciate it. See related Principle 34.

Ref: Kernighan, B., and P. Plauger, *The Elements of Programming Style*, New York: McGraw-Hill, 1978, pp. 124-134.

PRINCIPLE 95
COMMENT BEFORE YOU FINALIZE YOUR CODE

I've often heard programmers say, "Why should I bother commenting my code now? It'll only change!" We comment code to make the software easier to debug, test, and maintain. By commenting your code *while* coding (or beforehand, see Principle 96), it will be easier for you to debug the software.

As you debug your software, you will undoubtably find flaws. If a flaw is in your conversion from the algorithm to the code, you'll need to change only the code, not the comments. If the flaw is in your algorithm, you'll need to change both the comments and code. But how would you even know you had an algorithmic error unless you had comments?

Ref: Kernighan, B., and P. Plauger, *The Elements of Programming Style*, New York: McGraw-Hill, 1978, pp. 141-144.

PRINCIPLE 96
DOCUMENT *BEFORE* YOU START CODING

This advice will seem strange to some readers, but it becomes natural after being practiced for a while. Principle 95 explained why you should document your code before finishing it. Principle 96 goes one step further: You should document your code *before* starting to code!

After performing detailed design on a component [that is, documenting its external interface and its algorithm(s)], write your in-line comments. Most of these in-line comments will be nothing other than the previously documented interface and algorithm. Put these comments through the compiler to make sure you haven't done anything silly (like omitting a comment delimiter). Then convert each line of comment into a corresponding program segment. (*Note:* If you end up with one line of program per comment, you probably specified your algorithm with too much detail.) You'll find debugging goes a lot smoother.

Ref: McConnell, S., *Code Complete*, Redmond, Wash.: Microsoft Press, 1993, Sections 4.2-4.4.

PRINCIPLE 97
HAND-EXECUTE EVERY COMPONENT

It might take 30 minutes to execute a software component by hand with a few simple test cases. Do it! I am suggesting this in addition to, not in lieu of, the more thorough computer-based unit testing that is already being performed. What is the cost? Just 30 minutes. What is the alternative? Save 30 minutes now, proceed with unit, integration, and system testing. The system fails. Three to four person days are spent trying to isolate the cause of the failure. A half-dozen components are isolated as possible candidates. Each is given to its developers for further examination. Each candidate spends 30 minutes executing the component by hand with a few simple test cases. In short, 30 minutes are less than three to four person days plus 6×30 minutes.

Ref: Ledgard, H., *Programming Proverbs*, Rochelle Park, N.J.: Hayden Book Company, 1975, Proverb 21.

PRINCIPLE 98
INSPECT CODE

Inspection of software detailed design and code was first proposed by Michael Fagan in his paper entitled "Design and Code Inspections to Reduce Errors in Program Development" [*IBM Systems Journal, 15,* 3 (July 1976), pp. 182-211]. It can account for as many as 82 percent of all errors found in software. Inspection is *much* better than testing for finding errors. Define criteria for completing an inspection. Keep track of the types of errors found through inspection. Fagan's inspections consume approximately 15 percent of development resources with a net reduction in total development cost of 25 to 30 percent.

Your original project schedule should account for the time to inspect (and correct) every component. You might think that *your* project cannot tolerate such "luxuries." However, you should not consider inspection a luxury. Data has shown that you can even reduce the time to test by 50 to 90 percent. If that's not incentive, I don't know what could be. By the way, there is a wealth of support data and tips on how to do inspections well in the referenced book.

Ref: Grady, R., and T. VanSlack, "Key Lessons in Achieving Widespread Inspection Use," *IEEE Software, 11,* 4 (July 1994), pp. 46-57.

PRINCIPLE 99
YOU *CAN* USE UNSTRUCTURED LANGUAGES

Unstructured code violates Edsger Dijkstra's guidance to restrict control structures to IF-THEN-ELSE, DO-WHILE, DO-UNTIL, and CASE. Notice that it *is* possible to write structured code in languages without these structures, such as in assembly languages, by documenting the code with the structured control statements and restricting the use of GOTO's to implementing these structures only.

To do this, first write your algorithms using the control structures preceding. Next, convert these into in-line comments. Next, translate the comments into their equivalent programming language statements. GOTO's will appear, but they will be implementing the better constructs and will facilitate, not hamper, readability, maintainability, and provability.

Ref: McConnell, S., *Code Complete*, Redmond, Wash.: Microsoft Press, 1993, Section 17.6.

PRINCIPLE 100
STRUCTURED CODE IS NOT NECESSARILY GOOD CODE

The original definition of *structured programming* presented by Edsger Dijkstra was provided to facilitate program proving. The constructs he recommended (IF-THEN-ELSE, DO-WHILE, etc.) have now become so commonplace (though program proving has not) that their use is now called "programming" rather than "structured programming." It is important to note, however, that not all "structured" programs are good. One can write incredibly obscure programs that are still structured. Structure is almost a necessary, but far from a sufficient, condition for quality programming.

Ref: Yourdon, E., *How to Manage Structured Programming*, New York: Yourdon, Inc., 1976, Section 5.2.2.

PRINCIPLE 101
DON'T NEST TOO DEEP

Nesting IF-THEN-ELSE statements greatly simplifies programming logic. On the other hand, nesting them more than, say, three levels decreases their understandability considerably. The human mind is capable of remembering only a certain amount of logic before it becomes confused. A variety of simple techniques can be used to reduce nesting. See the following reference for examples and techniques.

Ref: McConnell, S., *Code Complete*, Redmond, Wash.: Microsoft Press, 1993, Section 17.4.

PRINCIPLE 102
USE APPROPRIATE LANGUAGES

Programming languages vary greatly in their ability to help you do your job. Your specific project or product goals will often dictate the appropriate language. The following guidelines are meant to be just that—guidelines, not gospel.

If your number one goal is portability, then use a language that has been demonstrated to be highly portable (such as C, FORTRAN, or COBOL). If your number one goal is fast development, then use a language that aids in such fast development (4GL's, Basic, APL, C, C++, or SNOBOL). If your number one goal is low maintenance, then use a language with many built-in, quality-inducing features (such as Ada or Eiffel). If your application requires a great use of character strings or complex data structures, select a language that supports them. If your product must be maintained by a group of existing maintainers who know language X, then use language X. Finally, if your customer says, "Thou shalt use language Y," then use language Y or you won't be in business long.

Ref: McConnell, S., *Code Complete*, Redmond, Wash.: Microsoft Press, 1993, Section 3.5.

PRINCIPLE 103
PROGRAMMING LANGUAGE IS NOT AN EXCUSE

Some projects are forced to use a less-than-ideal programming language. This might be caused by a desire to reduce maintenance costs ("All our maintainers know COBOL"), to program fast ("We have the highest productivity with C"), to ensure high reliability ("Ada programs are the most fail-safe"), or to achieve high execution speed ("Our applications are so time-critical, we need to use assembly language"). It is possible to write quality programs in *any* language. In fact, if you are a good programmer, you should be a good programmer in any language (Principle 104); a less-than-ideal language might make you work harder, though.

Ref: Yourdon, E., *How to Manage Structured Programming*, New York: Yourdon, Inc., 1976, Section 5.2.5.

PRINCIPLE 104
LANGUAGE KNOWLEDGE IS NOT SO IMPORTANT

Good programmers are good regardless of the language used. Poor programmers are poor regardless of the language used. Nobody is a "great C programmer" and a "poor Ada programmer." If they really are poor at Ada, they probably were not great at C! In addition, a really good programmer should be able to learn any new language easily. This is because a really good programmer understands and appreciates the *concepts* of quality programming, not just the syntactic and semantic idiosyncrasies of some programming language.

So the primary driver of language selection for a project should be appropriateness (Principle 102), not the surge of programmers who whine, "But all we know is C." If some quit because the project selected a different language, the project is probably better off!

Ref: Boehm, B., *Software Engineering Economics*, Englewood Cliffs, N.J.: Prentice Hall, 1981, Section 26.5.

PRINCIPLE 105
FORMAT YOUR PROGRAMS

The understandability of a program is greatly enhanced by using standard indentation protocols. Which protocol you choose to follow matters little, but, once you select it, use it consistently.

I follow the rule of keeping THEN's and ELSE's directly below their corresponding IF's, END's directly below the BEGIN's or DO's they correspond to, and so on. Thus,

```
IF _____
THEN       BEGIN
           _____
           _____
           _____
           END
ELSE       IF _____
           THEN_____
           ELSE_____
DO WHILE ( )
           _____
           _____
           _____
END DO;
```

See lots more examples in the reference. By the way, the only thing worse than inconsistent indentations is incorrect indentation (like aligning an ELSE with the wrong IF or THEN)! To prevent accidental misalignments, use any commercially available pretty printer.

Ref: McConnell, S., *Code Complete,* Redmond, Wash.: Microsoft Press, 1993, Chapter 18.

PRINCIPLE 106
DON'T CODE TOO SOON

Coding software is analogous to constructing a building. Both require much preliminary work. Constructing a building without a solid and stable concrete foundation will not work. Coding without a solid and stable foundation of requirements and design will not work. Think about how much more difficult it is to modify a building after the foundation is poured!

Don't be coerced into coding prematurely because management wants to see "progress." Be sure the requirements and design are correct and appropriate before baselining them and certainly before coding the final product. Incidentally, don't conclude from this principle that prototyping is bad (Principles 5, 10, 11, 12, and 13). There is nothing wrong with experimenting with coding long before requirements are baselined. Just don't consider it the final product. Manny Lehman adds a counterpoint to this principle: Don't code too late!

Ref: Berzins, V., and Luqi, *Software Engineering with Abstractions*, Reading, Mass.: Addison-Wesley, 1991, Section 1.5.

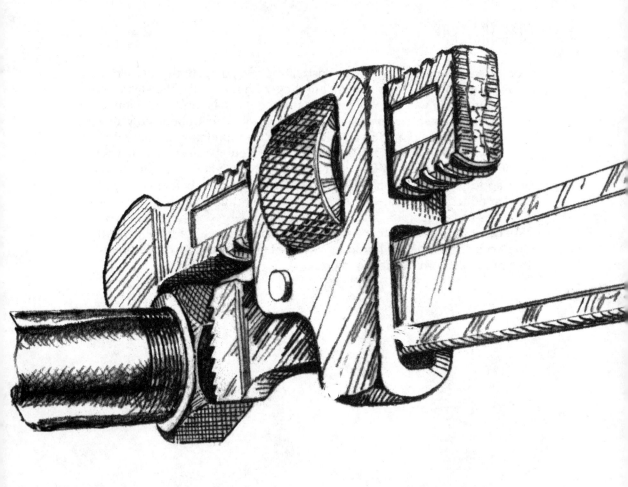

6 TESTING PRINCIPLES

Testing is a set of activities including:

1. Performing tests on individual software components (that is, unit testing) to conclude that they are sufficiently close to behaving as specified in the component's design specification.

2. Performing tests on sets of unit-tested components (integration testing) to conclude that they behave as a team in a manner close enough to how they were specified in the design.

3. Performing tests on the entirely integrated set of software components (software systems-level testing) to conclude that they behave as a system in a manner sufficiently close to that specified in the software requirements specification.

4. Generating test plans for software systems-level testing.

5. Generating test plans for software integration testing.

6. Generating test plans for unit testing.

7. Building test harnesses and test environments.

PRINCIPLE 107
TRACE TESTS TO REQUIREMENTS

It is important to understand which tests verify which requirements. There are two reasons: (1) When generating tests, you'll find it useful to know if all requirements are being tested. (2) When performing tests, you'll find it useful to know which requirements are being checked. Furthermore, if your requirements have been prioritized (Principle 50), you can easily derive the relative priorities of tests; that is, the priority of a test is the maximum of the priorities of all its corresponding requirements.

Maintain a large binary table in which rows correspond to all software tests and columns correspond to every requirement in the SRS. A 1 in any position indicates that this test helps to verify this requirement. Notice that a row void of 1's indicates that a test has no purpose and that a column void of 1's indicates an untested requirement. The successful creation of such a table depends on your ability to refer uniquely to every requirement (Principle 52).

Ref: Lindstrom, D., "Five Ways to Destroy a Development Project," *IEEE Software, 10,* 5 (September 1992), pp. 55-58.

PRINCIPLE 108
PLAN TESTS LONG BEFORE IT IS TIME TO TEST

Often software developers create their software product, then scratch their heads and say, "Now, how are we going to test this thing?" Test planning is a major task and must occur in parallel with product development so that test planning and initial (that is, pretesting) development activities are completed in synchrony.

For software system testing, test planners should review the SRS for testability before it is baselined and provide feedback to requirements writers. Serious development of the tests should start soon after baselining requirements. For integration testing, test planners should review the preliminary design before it is baselined. They should also provide feedback to the project managers and designers concerning (1) sensible allocations of resources to ensure that the "right" components (from a testing point of view) are produced in the right order and (2) modifications to the design to make it inherently easier to test. Serious integration test development should start soon after baselining the preliminary design. For unit testing, unit test plan development can start immediately after the completion of detailed design.

Ref: Goodenough, J., and S. Gerhart, "Toward a Theory of Test Data Selection," *IEEE Transactions on Software Engineering, 1,* 2 (June 1975), pp. 156-173, Section IIIC.

PRINCIPLE 109
DON'T TEST YOUR OWN SOFTWARE

Software developers should never be the primary testers of their own software. It is certainly appropriate to do initial debugging and unit testing. [For an opposing view, see Mills, H., et al., "Cleanroom Software Engineering," in *IEEE Software*, 4, 5 (September 1987), pp. 19-25.] Independent testers are necessary:

1. To check a unit for adequacy before starting integration testing.
2. For all integration testing.
3. For all software system testing.

The correct attitude during testing is that of wanting to expose bugs. How can a developer possibly embrace that attitude? Testing is difficult enough without burdening it further with testers who have a bias toward *not* finding bugs.

Ref: Myers, G., *The Art of Software Testing*, New York: John Wiley & Sons, 1979, p. 14.

PRINCIPLE 110
DON'T WRITE YOUR OWN TEST PLANS

Not only should you not test your own software (Principle 109), but you should also not be responsible for generating the test data, test scenarios, or test plans for your software. If you are, you may make the same mistakes in test generation that you made in software creation. For example, if you made a false assumption about the range of legal inputs when engineering the software, you would likely make the same assumption when generating test plans.

If you are a programmer and/or designer and your manager has asked you to write your test plans, I recommend you switch the test plan generation responsibility with a fellow programmer and/or designer. If you are a member of a requirements engineering team, with responsibility for system test generation as well, I recommend that members of your team subdivide the responsibilities so that no individual generates tests for requirements that she or he wrote.

Ref: Lehman, M., private communication, Colorado Springs, Col.: (January 24, 1994).

PRINCIPLE 111
TESTING EXPOSES PRESENCE OF FLAWS

No matter how thorough, testing simply exposes the presence of flaws in a program; it cannot be used to verify the absence of flaws. It can increase your confidence that a program is correct, but it cannot prove correctness. To gain true correctness, one must use completely different processes, that is, correctness proofs.

Ref: Dijkstra, E., "Notes on Structured Programming," in *Structured Programming*, Dahl, O., et al., eds., New York: Academic Press, 1972.

PRINCIPLE 112
THOUGH COPIOUS ERRORS GUARANTEE WORTHLESSNESS, ZERO ERRORS SAYS NOTHING ABOUT THE VALUE OF SOFTWARE

This is Gerald Weinberg's "Absence of Errors Fallacy." It really puts testing into perspective. It also puts all software engineering and management into perspective. The first part of the principle is obviously true; software with many errors is useless. The second part provides food for thought. It says that, no matter how hard you work to remove errors, you are wasting your time unless you are building the right system. Akao's *Quality Function Deployment* (Cambridge, Mass.: Productivity Press, 1990) provides details on one method of ensuring that you are building the right system throughout the life cycle. A corollary to this principle is that all the formal methods, all the testing, and all the product assurance in the world won't help if you are building the wrong system.

Ref: Weinberg, G., *Quality Software Management*, Vol. 1: Systems Thinking, New York: Dorset House, 1992, Section 12.1.2.

PRINCIPLE 113
A SUCCESSFUL TEST *FINDS* AN ERROR

I have often heard a tester gleefully declare, "Great news! My test was successful. The program ran correctly." This is the wrong attitude to have when running a test. [It also supports the position that programmers should never test their own software (Principle 109).] A more constructive attitude it that one is testing to *find* errors. Thus, a successful test is one that detects an error. Look at the analogous situation with a medical test. Suppose you are feeling ill. The physician sends a sample of your blood to a laboratory. A few days later, the physician calls to tell you, "Great news! Your blood was normal." That is not great news. You *are* sick or you wouldn't have gone to the physician. A successful blood test reports what's wrong with you. The software *has* bugs (or you wouldn't be testing it). A successful test reports how these bugs manifest themselves.

When generating test plans, you should select tests based on the likelihood that they will find faults. When testing software, the testing group should be evaluated on how well they find errors, not on how well they don't.

Ref: Goodenough, J., and S. Gerhart, "Toward a Theory of Test Data Selection," *IEEE Transactions on Software Engineering*, 1, 2 (June 1975), pp. 156-173.

PRINCIPLE 114
HALF THE ERRORS FOUND IN 15 PERCENT OF MODULES

Conservative estimates indicate that, in large systems, approximately half of all software errors are found in 15 percent of the modules, and 80 percent of all software errors are found in 50 percent of the modules. More dramatic results from Gary Okimoto and Gerald Weinberg indicate that 80 percent of all errors were found in just 2 percent of the modules (see Section 13.2.3 of Weinberg's *Quality Software Management*, Vol. 1: Systems Thinking, New York: Dorset House, 1992). Thus, when testing software, you might consider that, where you find errors, you will probably find more.

Maintain logs not only of how many errors are found per time period for the project, but also how many errors are found per module. When history shows a module to be highly error-prone, you are probably better off rewriting it from scratch, with an emphasis on simplicity (Principle 67) rather than cleverness.

Ref: Endres, A., "An Analysis of Errors and Their Causes in System Programs," *IEEE Transactions on Software Engineering, 1*, 2 (June 1975), pp. 140-149.

PRINCIPLE 115
USE BLACK-BOX AND WHITE-BOX TESTING

Black-box testing uses the specification of a component's external behavior as its only input. It is mandatory to determine if the software does what it is supposed to do and doesn't do what it is not supposed to do. *White-box testing* uses the code itself to generate test cases. Thus white-box testing might demand, for example, that all paths through the program of length 50 instructions or less be taken (Principle 122). Be aware, however, that even with both black-box and white-box testing, testing can make use of only a small subset of possible data values from the input domain (Principle 111).

To demonstrate how black-box and white-box testing complement each other, let's look at an example. Let's say a procedure's specification states that it should print the sum of all numbers in an input list. When programmed, it looks for one input of 213 and, if it finds it, sets the sum equal to zero. Since that was not in the specification, there is no way to find the error by black-box testing except by accident (that is, selecting a random test case that happens to include a 213). White-box testing would demand that paths are more adequately tested, and thus would probably detect the "213" situation. By combining black-box and white-box, you maximize the effectiveness of testing. Neither one by itself does a thorough test.

Ref: Dunn, R., *Software Defect Removal*, New York: McGraw-Hill, 1984, Section 7.4.

PRINCIPLE 116
A TEST CASE INCLUDES EXPECTED RESULTS

Documentation for a test case must include the detailed description of the expected correct results. If these are omitted, there is no way for the tester to determine whether the software succeeded or failed. Furthermore, a tester may assess an incorrect result as correct because there is always a subconscious desire to see a correct result. Even worse, a tester may assess a correct result as incorrect, causing a flurry of designer and coder activity to "repair" the correct code.

Develop an organization standard for test plans that demands the documentation of expected intermediate and final test case results. Your quality assurance organization should confirm that all test plans conform to the standard.

Ref: Myers, G., *The Art of Software Testing*, New York: John Wiley & Sons, 1979, p. 12.

PRINCIPLE 117
TEST INVALID INPUTS

It is natural and common to produce test cases for as many acceptable input scenarios as possible. What is equally important—but also uncommon—is to produce an extensive set of test cases for all invalid or unexpected inputs.

For a simple example, let us say we are writing a program to sort lists of integers in the range of 0 to 100. Test lists should include some negative numbers, all the same numbers, some nonintegral numbers, some alphabetic data, some null entries, and so on.

Ref: Myers, G., *The Art of Software Testing*, New York: John Wiley & Sons, 1979, p. 14.

PRINCIPLE 118
ALWAYS STRESS TEST

Software design often behaves just fine when confronted with "normal" loads of inputs or stimuli. The true test of software is whether it can stay operational when faced with severe loads. These severe loads are often stated in the requirements as "maximum of x simultaneous widgets" or "maximum of x new widget arrivals per hour."

If the requirements state that the software shall handle up to x widgits per hour, you must verify that the software can do this. In fact, not only should you test that it handles x widgits, you should also subject the software to $x+1$ or $x+2$ (or more) widgits to see what happens (Principle 58). After all, the system may not be able to control its environment, and you do not want the software to crash when the environment "misbehaves" in an unexpected manner.

Ref: Myers, G., *The Art of Software Testing*, New York: John Wiley & Sons, 1979, pp. 113-114.

PRINCIPLE 119
THE BIG BANG THEORY DOES NOT APPLY

As a project nears its delivery deadline and the software is not ready, desperation often takes over. Suppose the schedule called for two months of unit testing, two months of integration testing, and two months of software system testing. It is now one month from the scheduled delivery. Suppose 50 percent of the components have been unit-tested. A back-of-the-envelope calculation indicates that you are five months behind schedule. You have two choices:

1. Admit the five-month delay to your customer: Ask for a postponement.
2. Put all the components together (including the 50 percent not yet unit-tested) and hope for the best.

In the first case, you are admitting defeat, perhaps prematurely. In the eyes of your managers, you might be giving up before you've done everything in your power to overcome the problem. In the second case, there might be a .001 percent chance that, when you put it all together, it will work and you'll be back on schedule. Project managers often succumb to the latter because it looks like they are trying everything before admitting defeat. Unfortunately, this will probably add six *more* months to your schedule. You cannot save time by omitting unit and integration testing.

Ref: Weinberg, G., *Quality Software Management*, Vol. 1: Systems Thinking, New York: Dorset House, 1992, Section 13.2.3.

PRINCIPLE 120
USE McCABE COMPLEXITY MEASURE

Although many metrics are available to report the inherent complexity of software, none is as intuitive and as easy-to-use as Tom McCabe's cyclomatic number measure of testing complexity. Although not absolutely foolproof, it results in fairly consistent predictions of testing difficulty. Simply draw a graph of your program, in which nodes correspond to sequences of instructions and arcs correspond to nonsequential flow of control. McCabe's metric is simply $e-n+2p$ where e is the number of arcs, n is the number of nodes, and p is the number of independent graphs you are examining (usually 1). This metric can also be "calculated" by the cookie cutter analogy: Imagine pressing a cookie cutter shaped like the program graph into rolled-out dough. The number of cookies produced (the number of regions in the graph) is the same as $e-n+2p$. This is so simple that there is really no excuse not to use it.

Use McCabe on each module to help assess unit testing complexity. Also, use it at the integration testing level where each procedure is a node and each invocation path is an arc to help assess integration testing complexity.

Ref: McCabe, T., "A Complexity Measure," *IEEE Transactions on Software Engineering*, 2, 12 (December 1976), pp. 308-320.

PRINCIPLE 121
USE EFFECTIVE TEST COMPLETION MEASURES

Many projects proclaim the end of testing when they run out of time. This may make political sense, but it is irresponsible. During test planning, define a measure that can be used to determine when testing should be completed. If you have not met your goal when time runs out, you can still make the choice of whether to ship the product or slip the milestone, but at least *you* know whether you are shipping a quality product.

Two ideas for this effective measurement of test progress are:

1. Rate of new error detections per week.
2. After covertly seeding the software with known bugs (called *bebugging* by Tom Gilb), the percentage of these seeded bugs thus far found.

An ineffective measure of test progress is the percentage of test cases correctly passed (unless, of course, you *know* that the test cases are a superb cover of the requirements).

Ref: Dunn, R., *Software Defect Removal*, New York: McGraw-Hill, 1984, Section 10.3.

PRINCIPLE 122
ACHIEVE EFFECTIVE TEST COVERAGE

In spite of the fact that testing cannot prove correctness, it is still important to do a thorough job of testing. Metrics exist to determine how thoroughly the code was exercised during test plan generation or test execution. These metrics are easy to use, and tools exist to monitor the coverage level of tests. Some examples include:

1. Statement coverage, which measures the percentage of statements that have been executed at least once.
2. Branch coverage, which measures the percentage of branches in a program that have been executed.
3. Path coverage, which measures how well the possible paths (usually infinite) have been exercised.

Just remember that, although "effective" coverage is better than no coverage at all, do not fool yourself into thinking that the program is "correct" by *any* definition (Principle 111).

Ref: Weiser, M., J. Gannon, and P. McMullin, "Comparison of Structural Test Coverage Metrics," *IEEE Software, 2,* 2 (March 1985), pp. 80-85.

PRINCIPLE 123
DON'T INTEGRATE BEFORE UNIT TESTING

Under normal circumstances components are separately unit-tested. As they pass their unit tests, a separate organization integrates them into meaningful sets to exercise their interfaces. Components that have not been separately unit-tested are often integrated into the subsystem in a vein attempt to recapture a lost schedule. Such attempts actually cause more schedule delays. This is because a failure of a subsystem to satisfy an integration test plan may be caused now either by a fault in the interface or by a fault in the previously untested component. And much time is spent trying to determine which is the cause.

If you are managing a project, you can do a variety of things to avoid this situation. First and foremost is to develop an integration test plan early (for example, very soon after high-level design is complete). This plan should specify which components are most important to integrate first and in what order components may be integrated. Once you have written this down, allocate appropriate resources to coding and unit testing of specific high-priority components to ensure that integration testers don't spend an inordinate amount of time idle. Second, as it becomes evident that important components for integration testing are going to be unavailable as needed, have the integration testers start developing temporary *scaffolding software* to simulate the missing components.

Ref: Dunn, R., *Software Defect Removal*, New York: McGraw-Hill, 1984, Section 7.2.

PRINCIPLE 124
INSTRUMENT YOUR SOFTWARE

When testing software, it is often difficult to determine why the software failed. One way of uncovering the reasons is to instrument your software, that is, embed special instructions in the software that report traces, anomalous conditions, procedure calls, and the like. Of course, if your debugging system provides these capabilities, don't instrument manually.

Ref: Huang, J., "Program Instrumentation and Software Testing," *IEEE Computer, 11,* 4 (April 1978), pp. 25-32.

PRINCIPLE 125
ANALYZE CAUSES FOR ERRORS

Errors are common in software. We spend enormous amounts of resources detecting and fixing them. It is far more cost-effective to reduce their impact by preventing them from occurring in the first place. One way to do this is to analyze the causes for errors as they are detected. The causes are broadcast to all developers with the idea being that we are less apt to make an error of the same type as one whose cause was thoroughly analyzed and learned from.

When an error is detected there are two things to do: (1) Analyze its cause and (2) fix it. Record everything you can about the cause of the error. This is not just technical issues like, "I should have checked the passed parameter for validity before using it" or "I should have found out if I needed to execute the loop n or $n-1$ times before I gave it to integration testing." It is also management issues like, "I should have desk-checked before unit testing" or "If I had let Ellen check the design to see if it satisfied all the requirements when she wanted to, …" After collecting all this information, broadcast it, letting everybody know what caused the errors, so that such knowledge can become more widespread and such errors can become less widespread.

Ref: Kajihara, J., G. Amamiya, and T. Saya, "Learning from Bugs," *IEEE Software, 10,* 5 (September 1993), pp. 46-54.

PRINCIPLE 126
DON'T TAKE ERRORS PERSONALLY

Writing software requires a level of detail and perfection that no human can reach. We should dedicate ourselves to constant *improvement*, not perfection. When an error is detected in your code either by you or by others, discuss it openly. Instead of castigating yourself, use it as a learning experience for yourself and others (see more on this in Principle 125).

Ref: Gerhart, S., and L. Yelowitz, "Observations of Fallibility in Applications of Modern Programming Methodologies," *IEEE Transactions on Software Engineering*, 2, 3 (September 1976), pp. 195-207, Section I.

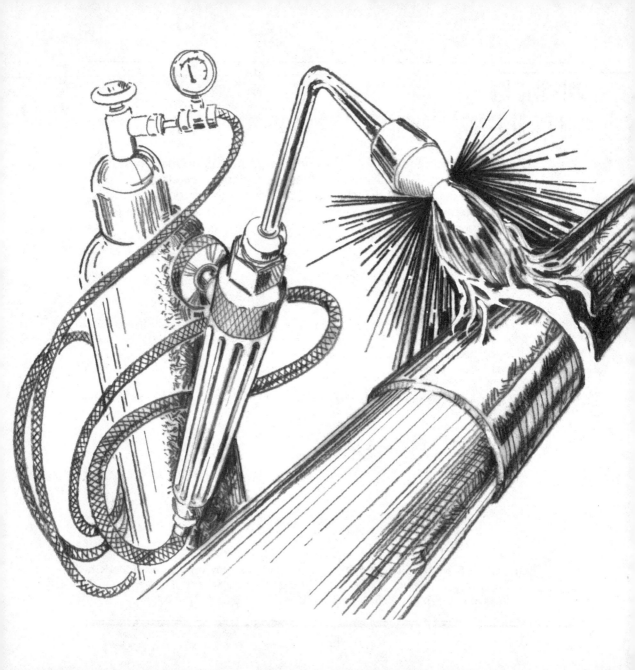

7 MANAGEMENT PRINCIPLES

Management is the set of activities for planning, controlling, monitoring, and reporting on all the engineering activities that encompass software development.

PRINCIPLE 127
GOOD MANAGEMENT IS MORE IMPORTANT THAN
GOOD TECHNOLOGY

Good management motivates people to do their best. Poor management demotivates people. All the great technology (CASE tools, techniques, computers, word processors, and the like) will not compensate for poor management. And good management can actually produce great results even with meager resources. Successful software startups do not become successful because they have great process or great tools (or great products for that matter!). Most have been successful because of great management and great marketing.

As a manager, you have a responsibility to be your best. There are no universally "right" styles of management. Management style must be adapted to the situation. It is not uncommon for a successful leader to be an autocrat in one situation and a consensus-based leader in another, just a few minutes later. Some styles are innate. Others *can* be learned. If necessary, read books and take short courses on management style.

Ref: Fenton, N., "How Effective Are Software Engineering Methods?" *Journal of Systems and Software, 22,* 2 (August 1993), pp. 141-146.

PRINCIPLE 128
USE APPROPRIATE SOLUTIONS

A technical problem needs a technical solution. A management problem needs a management solution. A political problem needs a political solution. Do not try to throw an inappropriate solution at a problem.

PRINCIPLE 129
DON'T BELIEVE EVERYTHING YOU READ

As a general rule, people who believe in a particular philosophy search for data that supports that philosophy and discard data that does not. Someone who wants to convince others of a position obviously uses supportive, not unsupportive, data. When you read, "Use method X. You too can achieve up to 93 percent increases in productivity (or quality)," the method may really have achieved such results. But it was probably the exceptional case. In all likelihood, most projects experience far less dramatic results. And some projects may even experience decreased productivity using method X.

Ref: Fenton, N., "How Effective Are Software Engineering Methods?" *Journal of Systems and Software*, 22, 2 (August 1993), pp. 141-146.

PRINCIPLE 130
UNDERSTAND THE CUSTOMERS' PRIORITIES

It is quite possible that the customers would rather have 90 percent of the system's functionality late if they could just have 10 percent of it on time. This corollary of Principle 8 is quite a bit more shocking, but it could very well be the case. Find out!

If you are communicating with your customers, you should be sure you know their priorities. These can easily be recorded in the requirements specification (Principle 50), but the real challenge is to understand the possibly ever shifting priorities. In addition, you must understand the customers' interpretation of "essential," "desirable," and "optional." Will they really be happy with a system that satisfies none of the desirable and optional requirements?

Ref: Gilb, T., "Deadline Pressure: How to Cope with Short Deadlines, Low Budgets and Insufficient Staffing Levels," in *Information Processing*, H.J. Kugler, ed., Amsterdam: Elsevier Publishers, 1986.

		Quality Managers and Engineers	
		Yes	No
Quality Processes, Tools, Languages	Yes	✓	✗
	No	✓	✗

PRINCIPLE 131
PEOPLE ARE THE KEY TO SUCCESS

Highly skilled people with appropriate experience, talent, and training are key to producing software that satisfies user needs on time and within the budget. The right people with insufficient tools, languages, and process *will* succeed. The wrong people (or the right people with insufficient training or experience) with appropriate tools, languages, and process will probably fail. According to COCOMO (Boehm, B., *Software Engineering Economics*, Englewood Cliffs, N.J.: Prentice Hall, 1984), the best people are four times more productive than others. If the best people cost four times the salary, you break even and probably end up with a better product (Principle 82). If they cost less, you reduce costs *and* have a better product. That's a win-win.

When interviewing prospective employees, remember that there is no substitute for quality. Companies often say, after interviewing two people, "Person x is better than person y, but person y is good enough and less expensive." You can't have an organization of all superstars, but, unless you have an overabundance of them now, hire them!

Ref: Weinberg, G., *The Psychology of Computer Programming*, New York: Van Nostrand Reinhold, 1971, Chapters 6-7.

PRINCIPLE 132
A FEW GOOD PEOPLE ARE BETTER THAN MANY LESS
SKILLED PEOPLE

This follows immediately from Principle 131, which says that you should always hire the best engineers. This principle says that you are better off allocating just a few good, experienced engineers on a critical task than to put many inexperienced engineers on it. This is Don Reifer's "Management Principle #6." On the other hand, Manny Lehman warns that you can't rely too much on "a few good people"; what if they quit? The best advice is to have the right mix of people on a project and take care not to gravitate toward either extreme.

Ref: Reifer, D., "The Nature of Software Management: A Primer," *Tutorial: Software Management*, D. Reifer, ed., Washington, D.C.: IEEE Computer Society Press, 1986, pp. 42-45.

PRINCIPLE 133
LISTEN TO YOUR PEOPLE

The people who work for you must be trusted. If they're not trustworthy (or if you don't trust them), your project will fail. If they don't trust you, your project will also fail. Your people can tell as quickly that you don't trust them as you can when your boss doesn't trust you.

The first rule of trust is listening. There are many opportunities to listen to your people: when they visit your office to tell you about a problem they are having, when you need an estimate from them for a software development, when you are managing by walking around (MBWA), among others. Whenever your people are talking to you, listen *and* hear. They consider what they are saying to be important or they wouldn't be telling you. There are many ways to let them know you are listening: eye contact, appropriate body language, "playing back" what you think you heard them say, asking appropriate questions to solicit more information, and so on.

Ref: Francis, P., *Principles of R&D Management*, New York: AMACOM, 1977, pp. 114-116.

PRINCIPLE 134
TRUST YOUR PEOPLE

In general, if you trust people, they will be trustworthy. If you treat people as if you don't trust them, they will give you reason not to trust them. When you trust others and give them no reason not to trust you, they will trust you. Mutual trust is essential for successful management.

When one of your employees says, "Can I take off today at 2 P.M.? I'll work a few hours extra later in the week," you should say, "Yes." You lose nothing, and you gain the loyalty and respect of your employee. There are many more opportunities to be the bad guy than the good guy. Take every chance you can get to be the good guy. Who knows, maybe in a few weeks you'll need to ask the employee to work a few extra hours for a job you need to have done.

Ref: McGregor, D., *The Human Side of Enterprise*, New York: McGraw-Hill, 1960.

PRINCIPLE 135
EXPECT EXCELLENCE

Your employees will do much better if you have high expectations of them. Studies by Warren Bennis prove conclusively that, the more you expect, the more results will be achieved (obviously with some limit). In many experiments, heterogeneous groups were divided into two subgroups with identical goals. One subgroup was treated as if excellence was expected. The other subgroup was treated as if mediocrity was expected. In every experiment, the group for whom excellence was expected outperformed the other group.

You can show in many ways that you expect excellence: Be an example (work hard, be proud of your efforts well done, don't play computer games on the job). Provide educational benefits to your employees to help them achieve their best. Reward excellent behavior (but see Principle 138). Coach, tutor, cajole, and attempt to inspire your poorer performers toward better work products and habits. If you (or they) fail, find more suitable opportunities for them within your organization or your company. If all else fails, help them find a job outside. You cannot allow them to stay in an inappropriate job, but you must also show compassion. If you leave them where they are, your product will be of lower quality and your other employees will assume that poor performance is acceptable.

Ref: Bennis, W., *The Unconscious Conspiracy: Why Leaders Can't Lead,* New York: AMA-COM, 1976.

PRINCIPLE 136
COMMUNICATION SKILLS ARE ESSENTIAL

When recruiting personnel for your project, don't underestimate the importance of teamwork and communication. The best designer becomes a poor asset if he/she is unable to communicate, convince, listen, and compromise.

Ref: Curtis, B., H. Krasner, and N. Iscoe, "A Field Study of the Software Design Process for Large Systems," *Communications of the ACM, 31,* 11 (November 1988), pp. 1268-1287.

PRINCIPLE 137
CARRY THE WATER

When your people are working long hours to get a software engineering job done, you should work the same hours. This sets the right example. Your employees will be more willing to work hard and do a good job if they know you are in the predicament with them. My first industrial manager, Tomlinson Rauscher, did precisely this. It made all the difference in our attitude. During crises, Tom took on the role of "working for his employees." It worked.

If you can't help with the engineering work itself, let them know you are available to run errands, order a pizza, bring them sodas, carry the water, whatever they need. Surprise them! Bring them a pizza at midnight.

Ref: Rauscher, T., private communication, 1977.

PRINCIPLE 138
PEOPLE ARE MOTIVATED BY DIFFERENT THINGS

This was perhaps the hardest lesson for me to learn as a manager. I assumed incorrectly that my employees were motivated by the same things that motivated me. I remember working hard one year with my raise pool to allocate raises fairly. I wanted especially to give very large raises to specific employees to reward them for a great job and to motivate them to work even harder. When I presented the first raise, the employee said, "Thanks, but what I really need is a faster computer."

Sometimes it is not so easy to find out which carrots and which sticks motivate individuals. What is known is that people are all different, that negative and positive reinforcements both work, but that positive reinforcements are more often neglected by management. A good way to start figuring out what motivates individual people is to listen to them (Principle 133). The rest might be by trial and error. But whatever you do, don't suppress rewards out of fear of selecting the wrong one.

Ref: Herzberg, F., "One More Time: How Do You Motivate Employees?" *Harvard Business Review* (September-October 1987).

PRINCIPLE 139
KEEP THE OFFICE QUIET

The most productive employees and companies have quiet and private offices. They have phones that can be silenced or diverted. They are insulated from regular, nonbusiness interruptions. Contrast this with the general industry movement toward open, landscaped offices, which reduce physical plant cost but dramatically decrease productivity and quality. Of course, the usual management line is that such an arrangement "facilitates communication." Not true. It "facilitates interruption and noise."

Ref: DeMarco, T., and T. Lister, *Peopleware*, New York: Dorset House, 1987, Chapter 12.

PRINCIPLE 140
PEOPLE AND TIME ARE NOT INTERCHANGEABLE

Measuring a project solely by person-months makes little sense. If a project could be completed in one year by six people, does that mean that 72 people could complete it in one month? Of course not!

Suppose you have 10 people working on a project that is due for completion in three months. You now believe you are three months behind schedule; that is, you estimate you need 60 more person-months (6 months × 10 people). You cannot add 10 more people and expect the project to be back on schedule. In fact, adding 10 more people would likely delay the project further due to additional training and communications overhead. This principle is usually called Brooks' Law.

Ref: Brooks, F., *The Mythical Man-Month*, Reading, Mass.: Addison-Wesley, 1975, Chapter 2.

PRINCIPLE 141
THERE ARE HUGE DIFFERENCES AMONG SOFTWARE ENGINEERS

Productivity (measured by lines of code per person-month) can vary by as much as a factor of 25 from the best to the worst software engineers. Quality (measured by bugs found per thousand lines of code) can vary by as much as a factor of 10 from the best to the worst software engineers.

Ref: Sackman, H., et al., "Exploratory Experimental Studies Comparing Online and Offline Programming Performance," *Communications of the ACM, 11,* 1 (January 1968), pp. 3-11.

PRINCIPLE 142
YOU CAN OPTIMIZE WHATEVER YOU WANT

Any project can optimize whatever factor of "quality" it wants to. In optimizing any one factor, other "quality" factors are generally denigrated. In a landmark experiment conducted by G. Weinberg and E. Schulman, five teams of software developers were given identical requirements, but each was told to optimize something different: development time, program size, data space used, program clarity, and user friendliness. In all cases except one the programs produced by the teams were rated best in terms of the attribute they were told to optimize.

If you tell your people that everything (such as schedule, size, maintainability, performance, and user friendliness) is equally important, none will be optimized. If you tell them that only one or two are important and the rest unimportant, only the important ones will be addressed. If you give them an a priori relative ranking, the ranking may not be appropriate in all situations on the project. The fact is that there are trade-offs—different trade-offs—to be made constantly during product development. Work *with* your employees and help them understand your priorities and your customers'.

Ref: Weinberg, G., and E. Schulman, "Goals and Performance in Computer Programming," *Human Factors, 16* (1974), pp. 70-77.

PRINCIPLE 143
COLLECT DATA UNOBTRUSIVELY

Data collection is extremely important to help with future cost predictions, to assess the current state of a project or organization, to assess the effect of a change in management, process, or technology, and so on. On the other hand, data collection in an obtrusive fashion—for example, if it requires software developers to do considerably extra work—is meaningless because its collection affects the data itself. Furthermore, data collected from developers who do not want to provide such data will likely be useless because it is unlikely that an uncooperative developer will provide meaningful data.

The best way to collect data is automatically, with no developer-perceived interference. Obviously you cannot do this all the time for all data, but you should automate data collection whenever you can.

Ref: Pfleeger, S., "Lessons Learned in Building a Corporate Metrics Program," *IEEE Software, 10,* 3 (May 1993), pp. 67-74.

PRINCIPLE 144
COST PER LINE OF CODE IS NOT USEFUL

Given a particular set of requirements, we may choose to implement the program in any of numerous languages. If we choose a very high-level language, we will spend much less time than if we choose a very low-level language (Principle 152). Thus total development costs will be far less when using the high-level language. However, because of the fixed costs of software development (such as user documentation, requirements, and design), the cost per line of code actually increases if we choose the high-level language! Capers Jones explains this well with an analogy to manufacturing: As the number of units produced decreases, the cost per unit increases because the fixed costs must now be absorbed by a smaller set of units.

Ref: Jones, C., *Programming Productivity*, New York: McGraw-Hill, 1986, Chapter 1.

PRINCIPLE 145
THERE IS NO PERFECT WAY TO MEASURE PRODUCTIVITY

The two most commonly used ways of defining productivity are source lines of code (SLOC) and function points (FP) per person-month. Both have problems. Measuring SLOCs looks good at first glance because, in most engineering or manufacturing fields, producing more is better. However, if you have two programs that do the same thing, one is twice the size of the other, and both exhibit the same qualities (except for size, of course), then the smaller one is better. Function points seem to solve the problem because they measure the complexity of the problem (through the analysis of requirements specification) rather than the solution. But here too there is a problem. Suppose two requirements specifications are identical in every way except one says, "If the system crashes, all of humanity will be destroyed" and the other says, "If the system crashes, two five-year-olds will be slightly inconvenienced." Clearly the former is a much more difficult problem and thus should exhibit far lower productivity than the latter. There are published techniques to convert a LOC estimate into an FP estimate, and vice versa. Clearly, neither can have a consistent advantage over the other.

Accept the fact that perfection is impossible. Use productivity measures and cost estimation models to confirm your intuition and your own experiences. Never rely on them as your sole measure.

Ref: Fairley, R., "Recent Advances in Software Estimation Techniques," *14th IEEE International Conference on Software Engineering,* Washington, D.C.: IEEE Computer Society Press, 1992.

PRINCIPLE 146
TAILOR COST ESTIMATION METHODS

Numerous cost estimation methods are available commercially. Each is based on data collected from a large set of completed projects. Any of these methods can be used to generate ball park estimates for your software development. To use them to generate more accurate estimates, you must tailor them to your work environment. This tailoring adapts the model to your type of people and your type of applications. It eliminates variables that are invariant in your environment. It adds variables that are productivity-influential in your environment.

Chapter 29 of Barry Boehm's *Software Engineering Economics* explains in detail how to tailor COCOMO to your environment. Similar tailoring guidance is provided with other cost estimation methods. You must fully embrace the spirit of such tailoring, or you will end up with dismally inaccurate results.

Ref: Boehm, B., *Software Engineering Economics,* Englewood Cliffs, N.J.: Prentice Hall, 1981, Section 29.9.

PRINCIPLE 147
DON'T SET UNREALISTIC DEADLINES

It is a foregone conclusion that an unrealistic deadline will not be met. The establishment of such deadlines erodes morale, causes your fellow employees to distrust you, creates high employee turnover, and has other undesirable effects. These factors then make the unrealistic deadline even more unachievable. A large majority of software projects are completed well over budget and well beyond the scheduled completion date. In an effort to meet schedule constraints, quality is often reduced. This erodes the credibility of the entire software industry. The problem is generally not that the software engineers have poor productivity or that managers do a poor job managing. The problem is that poor estimates are made up front.

Ref: DeMarco, T., "Why Does Software Cost So Much?" *IEEE Software,* 10, 2 (March 1993), pp. 89-90.

PRINCIPLE 148
AVOID THE IMPOSSIBLE

This may seem like obvious advice. On the other hand, many projects commit to delivering their product on schedules that are 100 percent impossible. Barry Boehm has defined the "impossible region" as a relationship between the expected time to develop a product and the number of person-months to be consumed. Specifically, the elapsed time from writing a software requirements specification to product delivery will not be less than 2.15 times the cube root of person-months, that is,

$$T > 2.15\sqrt[3]{PM}$$

Ninety-nine percent of all completed projects have obeyed this rule. What makes you think you can do better? If you still think you can, see Principles 3, 19, 158, and 159.

Ref: Boehm, B., *Software Engineering Economics*, Englewood Cliffs, N.J.: Prentice Hall, 1981, Section 27.3.

PRINCIPLE 149
KNOW BEFORE YOU COUNT

Gerald Weinberg (*Rethinking Systems Analysis and Design*, New York: Dorset House, 1988, p. 32) states this principle beautifully: "Before you can count anything, you've got to know something." He is talking about the many people who count things in software but don't know what they are counting. He provides a great example. We have data concerning what percentage of the software industry is involved with maintenance rather than development. But can we recognize maintenance? Is a "new" development that completely replaces an existing system considered maintenance or development? Is a "modification" to an existing system that doubles current functionality and removes 95 percent of old functionality considered maintenance or development?

When selecting metrics for your project, make sure that what you are measuring relates to what you are trying to achieve. (See the opening paragraphs of my Manager Column in the September 1993 *IEEE Software* for a personal testimony.) This often entails using multiple metrics. Remember: Even if everybody is measuring something one way, that way is not automatically right for you. *Think* about your metrics. Since everything *can* be observed (and in most cases measured), carefully select what you want to observe (and measure). The article referenced below is the best description I've seen of an organization-tailored metrics program.

Ref: Stark, G., R. Durst, and C. Vowell, "Using Metrics in Management Decision-Making," *IEEE Computer, 27,* 9 (September 1994).

PRINCIPLE 150
COLLECT PRODUCTIVITY DATA

The accuracy of all cost estimation models is dependent on the tailoring of those models for *your* workplace. But you cannot tailor your cost estimation models today if you haven't already collected detailed data from past projects. You therefore have a great excuse not to do accurate cost estimations now. But what about tomorrow? You will not be able to tailor cost estimation models then if you don't start collecting detailed data today. So what are you waiting for? Also remember Manny Lehman's advice: A little data that is well understood and carefully collected, modeled, and interpreted is better than a vast amount of data without these properties.

Ref: Boehm, B., *Software Engineering Economics*, Englewood Cliffs, N.J.: Prentice Hall, 1981, Section 32.7.

PRINCIPLE 151
DON'T FORGET *TEAM* PRODUCTIVITY

It is relatively easy to decide on a set of productivity measures for individuals. (Of course, they may not yield accurate results, as highlighted by Principles 142, 144, and 145.) However, be aware that optimizing the productivity of all individuals does not necessarily result in optimal productivity of the team. Compare this to a basketball team. Every player can optimize her/his own performance by always shooting for the basket when in possession of the ball. However, the team will surely lose. Manny Lehman reports on one software development effort in which individual productivity tripled but corporate productivity actually decreased!

There are two lessons to be learned here: First, different measures are appropriate for different people. Second, measure the overall effectiveness of the team by tracking such things as the team's ability to resolve outstanding problem reports by problem difficulty, per time period.

Ref: Lehman, M., private communication, Colorado Springs, Col.: (January 25, 1994).

PRINCIPLE 152
LOC/PM INDEPENDENT OF LANGUAGE

It is generally believed that a programmer can generate on the average x lines of quality code per person-month regardless of the language being used. Thus, if a programmer can generate 500 lines of quality code per month in Ada, that person could also generate 500 lines of quality code per month in assembly language. For an opposing viewpoint, see C. Jones, *Programming Productivity* (New York: McGraw-Hill, 1986, Chapter 1). True productivity, of course, is greatly enhanced when using higher-level languages because 500 lines of Ada code do so much more than 500 lines of assembler. Furthermore, language selection greatly affects maintainability (Principle 193).

When starting a project you will need to have some idea of what language your programmers will be using. This is necessary so that you can estimate the lines of code. Lines of code can then be used to compute project effort and duration.

Ref: Boehm, B., *Software Engineering Economics*, Englewood Cliffs, N.J.: Prentice Hall, 1981, Section 33.4.

| | | Realism of Schedule | |
	Realistic	Constrained	Very Constrained
Team Believes in Schedule Yes	Hi	Medium	Low
No	Low	Low	Low

PRINCIPLE 153
BELIEVE THE SCHEDULE

Once a feasible schedule is established (Principles 146, 147, and 148) and appropriate resources allocated (Principle 157), all parties must believe the schedule. Engineers will not succeed in meeting a schedule if they don't believe it is realistic. The probability of success is more a function of faith in the schedule than its realism.

The best advice is to have engineers set schedules. Unfortunately, this is not always possible. The second best advice is to involve engineers in the tough trade-offs that occur between functionality, schedule, and project abandonment. Few engineers would rather lose their job because a project is canceled than strive to meet a tough schedule.

Ref: Lederer, A., and J. Prasad, "Nine Management Guidelines for Better Cost Estimating," *Communications of the ACM, 35,* 2 (February 1992), pp. 51-59, Guideline 1.

PRINCIPLE 154
A PRECISION-CRAFTED COST ESTIMATE IS NOT FOOLPROOF

Suppose your organization has collected reams of data on past performance. Suppose you have tailored one of the many cost estimation models to your organization's capabilities based on this data. Suppose you are a project manager. You have a new project and you use this tailored model. The model reports that the software will cost $1 million. What does that mean? It does not mean your software will cost $1 million.

There are three reasons: (1) you, (2) assumptions, and (3) probability. First of all: You. Your leadership abilities will have a major effect on actual results. For example, in five seconds you can destroy the morale of your group that took a year to build. Second, all the assumptions you made to generate the initial estimate may not turn out to be accurate. For example, what if you get less qualified people? What if requirements change? What if your key person becomes ill? What if half your workstations go down when you need them the most? Third, the estimate is just a peak in a probabilistic distribution. If I tell you I'm going to toss a coin 100 times and ask you to predict how many times it will be heads, you'll probably pick 50. Does that mean 50 heads will appear? Of course not. In fact, you would be amazed if 50 heads appeared!

Ref: Gilb, T., *Principles of Software Engineering Management*, Reading, Mass.: Addison-Wesley, 1988, Section 16.7.

PRINCIPLE 155
REASSESS SCHEDULES REGULARLY

Schedules are usually set at project initiation. These include intermediate deadlines as well as the product delivery deadline. As each phase is completed, the schedule must be reassessed. A behind-schedule project rarely recovers during subsequent phases. Thus, a project that is, say, one month late at completion of design will be at least one month late for delivery. In most cases adding or removing people will only delay the project further (Principle 140). The most common technique is not to change the product delivery date. (After all, we don't want to disappoint the customer just yet, do we?) As each intermediate milestone is missed by an increasing amount of time, the time allocated to testing is reduced more and more (Principle 119). At the end, one of two situations is inevitable: (1) The product is shipped without the necessary quality, or (2) the customer is notified of a very large schedule slip very late in the project. Neither is acceptable. As a manager, your responsibility is to *prevent* disasters.

Instead, establish a working relationship with customers and/or management levels above you. Report every possible date change (usually a slip) and discuss the alternative strategies for overcoming them. Only early intervention and involvement by all parties can prevent slippage escalation.

Ref: Gilb, T., *Principles of Software Engineering Management*, Reading, Mass.: Addison-Wesley, 1988, Section 7.14.

PRINCIPLE 156
MINOR UNDERESTIMATES ARE NOT ALWAYS BAD

Assuming morale has not been diminished, members of a project that is perceived as slightly behind schedule will tend to work hard at catching up, thus increasing productivity. Similarly, members of a project that is perceived as slightly ahead of schedule often take vacation days, work less hours, read their mail longer, and ease up in other ways, thus decreasing productivity. Thus, the cost estimation itself will affect the project outcome. Any specific project may expend less resources if it is slightly underestimated than if it is slightly overestimated. Be careful, though! If project members believe that the schedule is ridiculously underestimated, morale and productivity will decrease.

Ref: Abdel-Hamid, T., and S. Madnick, "Impact on Schedule Estimation on Software Project Behavior," *IEEE Software, 3,* 4 (July 1986), pp. 70-75.

	Appropriate Schedules, Budgets and Resources	
	Yes	No
Quality Personnel, Process, Tools, Languages — Yes	✓	✗
Quality Personnel, Process, Tools, Languages — No	✗	✗

PRINCIPLE 157
ALLOCATE APPROPRIATE RESOURCES

Artificially constrained schedules and inappropriate budgets will doom a project regardless of the quality of the people or the availability of tools, languages, and process.

If you try to compress either schedule or budget, the engineers working on the project will not work efficiently, there will be no "play" when the inevitable slippage occurs, morale will suffer, and, most importantly, the project will probably cost more than what would otherwise be considered reasonable anyway.

Ref: DeMarco, T., "Why Does Software Cost So Much?" *IEEE Software, 10,* 2 (March 1993), pp. 89-90.

PRINCIPLE 158
PLAN A PROJECT IN DETAIL

Every software project needs a plan. The level of detail should be appropriate for the size and complexity of the project. At an absolute minimum, you will need:

- A PERT chart showing the interdependencies among tasks.
- A GANTT chart showing when activity will be underway on each task.
- A list of realistic milestones (based on earlier projects, see Principle 150).
- A set of standards for writing documentation and code.
- An allocation of people to various tasks.

As projects increase in complexity, each of these requirements becomes more detailed and more complex, and other documentation becomes necessary. A project without a plan is out of control before it even starts. As the Cheshire Cat said to Alice in Wonderland, "If you don't know where you are going, any road will get you there!"

Ref: Glaser, G., "Managing Projects in the Computer Industry," *IEEE Computer, 17,* 10 (October 1984), pp. 45-53.

PRINCIPLE 159
KEEP YOUR PLAN UP-TO-DATE

This is Don Reifer's "Management Principle #3." Principle 158 says that you must plan a software project. However, having an out-of-date plan is even worse than having no plan at all. When you have no plan, you should know you are out of control. When you have an out-of-date plan, you may naively think you are under control. So whenever circumstances change, update your plan. Such circumstances include changes to the requirements, a schedule slippage, a change in direction, finding excessive errors, or any deviation from the original conditions.

A well-written plan should enumerate the risks, the warning signs that the potential risk is becoming a threat, and contingency plans to put into place to reduce the threat (Principle 162). As a project progresses and predicted risks become threats, the contingency plans are implemented and the project plan is updated. The real challenge occurs when unforeseen changes occur. For these times, one often needs to replan the remainder of a project in its entirety, with new assumptions, new risks, new contingency plans, new schedules, new milestones, new person power loading, and so on.

Ref: Reifer, D., "The Nature of Software Management: A Primer," *Tutorial: Software Management*, D. Reifer, ed., Washington, D.C.: IEEE Computer Society Press, 1986, pp. 42-45.

PRINCIPLE 160
AVOID STANDING WAVES

One of the odd side-effects of following Principle 159 (Keep Your Plan Up-to-Date) is the standing wave. In this situation, you always plan the "get well" strategy to occur "over the next few weeks." Since projects that are behind schedule tend to get further behind schedule, this "get well" strategy requires larger and larger resources (or miracles!) to be applied "over the next few weeks." The wave gets larger and larger with no corrective action taken. Rescheduling and replanning in general require action, not just promises that things will be fixed soon. Just because you are only a few days behind, don't think the problem will go away. All projects "fall behind one day at a time."

Ref: Brooks, F., *The Mythical Man-Month*, Reading, Mass.: Addison-Wesley, 1975, Chapter 4.

PRINCIPLE 161
KNOW THE TOP 10 RISKS

As you start a project as a project manager, become familiar with the situations that most often cause software disasters. These are your most likely risks, but probably not all of them. According to Boehm, they are:

- Personnel shortfalls (Principle 131).
- Unrealistic schedules (Principle 148).
- Not understanding the requirements (Principle 40).
- Building a poor user interface (Principle 42).
- Trying to gold-plate when the customer doesn't want it (Principle 67).
- Not controlling requirements changes (Principles 179 and 189).
- Shortfalls of reusable or interfaced components.
- Shortfalls in externally performed tasks.
- Poor response time.
- Attempting to exceed the capability of current computer technology.

Now that you know the most common risks, add to them risks unique to your environment and project, and develop plans on how to mitigate them.(Principle 162.)

Ref: Boehm, B., "Software Risk Management: Principles and Practices," *IEEE Software, 9,* 1 (January 1991), pp. 32-39.

PRINCIPLE 162
UNDERSTAND RISKS UP FRONT

On any software project it is impossible to predict exactly what will go wrong. However, something will go wrong. In the early stages of planning, delineate the largest risks associated with your project. For each, quantify the extent of the damage if the risk potential becomes a project reality and also quantify the likelihood that this will come to pass. The product of these two numbers is your risk exposure with respect to that particular risk.

At project inception, construct a decision tree that delineates all the things you could do to lower the exposure. Then either act on the results immediately, or develop plans to implement various actions at points when the exposure exceeds your acceptable limits. (Of course, specify in advance how you will recognize this situation so that you can implement the corrective action before it is too late.)

Ref: Charette, R., *Software Engineering Risk Analysis and Management*, New York: McGraw-Hill, 1989, Section 2.2, Chapter 6.

PRINCIPLE 163
USE AN APPROPRIATE PROCESS MODEL

Dozens of process models are available for software projects to utilize: waterfall, throwaway prototyping, incremental development, spiral model, operational prototyping, to name but a few. There is no such thing as a process model that works for all projects in an organization. Every project must select a process that makes the most sense for it. The selection should be based on corporate culture, risk willingness, application area, volatility of requirements, and the extent to which requirements are well understood.

Study your project's characteristics and select a process model that makes the most sense. For example, when building a prototype, you should follow a process that minimizes protocol, facilitates rapid development, and does not worry about checks and balances. When building a life-critical product, the opposite is true.

Ref: Alexander, L., and A. Davis, "Criteria for the Selection of a Software Process Model," *IEEE COMPSAC '91*, Washington, D.C.: IEEE Computer Society Press, pp. 521-528.

PRINCIPLE 164
THE METHOD WON'T SAVE YOU

You have all heard the preachings of "method zealots" who say, "If you just adopt my method, most of your problems will disappear." Although many methods have been the subject of such ravings, the majority during the 1970s and early 1980s contained the word "structured" in their names and those during the late 1980s and 1990s contained "object" in their names. Although both of these waves bring great insights, as well as quality-instilling software development constructs and steps, they are not panaceas. Organizations that are really good at developing quality software were good before the "structured" methods and are good now when using "object-oriented" methods. Organizations with poor records will still have poor records after adopting the latest fad method.

As a manager, beware of false soothsayers who will promise great increases in either quality or productivity based on a new method. There is nothing wrong with adopting a new method, but if the organization has "failed" in the past (either in terms of productivity or quality), try to uncover the source of that failure before you jump to a solution. It is highly unlikely that your method is to blame!

Ref: Loy, P., "The Method Won't Save You (But It Can Help)," *ACM Software Engineering Notes, 18,* 1 (January 1993), pp. 30-34.

PRINCIPLE 165
NO SECRETS FOR MIRACULOUS PRODUCTIVITY INCREASES

This industry is saturated with salespeople who preach the reduction of development cost through the use of this tool or that technique. We all hear at business meetings and conferences about software managers claiming 50 percent, 75 percent, even 100 percent increases in productivity by applying tool x or language y or method z. Don't believe it! This is hype. The software industry is experiencing moderate (3 to 5 percent/year) increases in productivity. The fact is that we have a trivial way to reduce the cost of requirements engineering: Just don't do it! The same is true of all other phases. In fact, we can save lots of money by simply not building software!

You should be happy with tools, languages, and methods that shave a few percentages off your cost or add a few percentages to your quality. However, cost reduction makes no sense without an understanding of its impact on customer satisfaction.

Ref: DeMarco, T., and T. Lister, *Peopleware*, New York: Dorset House, 1987, Chapter 6.

PRINCIPLE 166
KNOW WHAT PROGRESS MEANS

I often hear project managers report, "We are 25 percent below budget" or "25 percent ahead of schedule." Neither is necessarily good news. "Below budget" usually means you spent less money than expected. That *could* be good, but you don't know unless you are also on or ahead of schedule. Similarly, "ahead of schedule" usually means you did more than you expected. That *could* be good news, but you don't know unless you are also on or below budget. There *are* meaningful measures of progress:

BCWP	"Budgeted cost of work performed" measures how much you expected to spend on work so far completed.
ACWP	"Actual cost of work performed" measures how much has actually been spent on the project.
BCWE	"Budgeted cost of work expected" measures how much you expected to spend.
$\dfrac{\text{BCWP-BCWE}}{\text{BCWE}}$	This captures true technical status. Greater-than-zero values indicate the percentage you are ahead of schedule. Less-than-zero values indicate the percentage behind schedule.
$\dfrac{\text{BCWP-ACWP}}{\text{BCWP}}$	This captures true budgetary status. Greater-than-zero values indicate the percentage under budget. Less-than-zero values indicate the percentage over budget.

Ref: U.S. Air Force, *Cost/Schedule Management of Non-Major Contracts,* Air Force Systems Command Publication #178-3, Andrews AFB, Md.: (November 1978).

PRINCIPLE 167
MANAGE BY VARIANCE

First of all, it is impossible to manage a project without a detailed plan (Principle 158). Once you have a plan, update it as necessary (Principle 159). Now that you have an up-to-date plan, your responsibility is to manage the project according to that plan. As you report your progress (it doesn't matter if this is written, oral, formal, or informal), report only discrepancies between the plan and the actuals. Project managers typically spend a large majority of the time reporting how well they are doing. There will be plenty of time at project completion for kudos. While the project is underway, a progress report should be, "Everything is as stated in the plan except ...." This way attention and resources can be applied to the problem areas.

PRINCIPLE 168
DON'T OVERSTRAIN YOUR HARDWARE

Be aware of the astronomical effect hardware constraints will have on software development costs. In particular, data shows that, as you approach 90 percent utilization of either memory or CPU cycles, software development costs *double*! And as you approach 95 percent, it *triples*! With the astronomical decreases in cost per instruction per second and cost per word of memory, this tends to be less of a problem than it was 15 years ago. On the other hand, there is still a strong motivation to control hardware cost in many applications (such as low-cost products that will be sold in vast quantities).

If memory is easy to add and faster processors are easily incorporated in your environment, do not worry about this principle; just add more when needed. If your environment is such that you must squeeze every word of memory and CPU cycle, then be sure to expand your schedules accordingly.

Ref: Boehm, B., "The High Cost of Software," in *Practical Strategies for Developing Large Software Systems*, E. Horowitz, ed., Reading, Mass.: Addison-Wesley, 1975.

PRINCIPLE 169
BE OPTIMISTIC ABOUT HARDWARE EVOLUTION

In 1984, 13 major aerospace corporations predicted that 50 percent of all software development would still be done on dumb terminals in 1988. By 1988, most software development had been taken off dumb terminals and transferred to PCs and workstations. In the same survey, they predicted only 15 percent of all software development environments would use Ethernet, and there would be only a 27 percent penetration of UNIX-based machines in software environments. Clearly, these predictions were all wrong. Hardware speed, capability, standardization, and price/performance all exceeded the predictions.

Ref: Davis, A., and E. Comer, "No Crystal Ball in the Software Industry," *IEEE Software,* *10,* 4 (July 1993), pp. 91-94, 97.

PRINCIPLE 170
BE PESSIMISTIC ABOUT SOFTWARE EVOLUTION

In 1984, 13 major aerospace corporations predicted that, by 1988, 46 percent of all their software development would be in Ada (and less than 4 percent in C), and that 54 percent of all their software would be reused from previous applications. Also, by 1994, 70 percent of all software development would be assisted by knowledge-based systems. None of these predictions has come to pass. In all cases, the technology either was too immature or was overtaken by events.

Ref: Davis, A., and E. Comer, "No Crystal Ball in the Software Industry," *IEEE Software,* *10,* 4 (July 1993), pp. 91-94, 97.

PRINCIPLE 171
THE THOUGHT THAT DISASTER IS IMPOSSIBLE OFTEN LEADS
TO DISASTER

This is Gerald Weinberg's "Titanic Effect" principle. You must never become so smug that you think everything is under control and will remain that way. Overconfidence is the primary cause of many disasters. It is the mountain climber who says, "It's just a small climb; I don't need a belay," or the hiker who says, "It's just a short hike; I don't need water," or the poker player who says, "This hand is a sure winner" who gets into trouble. Principle 162 emphasizes the need to analyze all your potential disasters up front, develop contingency plans for them in advance, and continually reassess new risks. This principle emphasizes the need to expect these risks to become real. Your biggest management disasters will occur when you think they won't.

Ref: Weinberg, G., *Quality Software Management*, Vol. 1: Systems Thinking, New York: Dorset House, 1992, Section 15.3.5.

PRINCIPLE 172
DO A PROJECT POSTMORTEM

Those who do not remember the past are condemned
to relive it.

George Santayana, 1908

Every project has problems. Principle 125 dealt with recording, analyzing, and learning from technical errors. This principle deals with doing the same for management or overall technical errors. At the end of every project, give all the key project players a three- or four-day assignment to analyze every problem that occurred during the project. For example, "We were 10 days late starting integration testing; we should have told the customer." Or, "We started the design long before we knew even the most basic of requirements." Or, "The big boss demotivated the people with a 'no raises' announcement at just the wrong time." In general, the idea is to document, analyze, and learn from all the things that went wrong. Also, record what you believe could be done differently in the future to prevent it. Future projects will benefit greatly.

Ref: Chikofsky, E., "Changing Your Endgame Strategy," *IEEE Software, 7*, 6 (November 1990), pp. 87, 112.

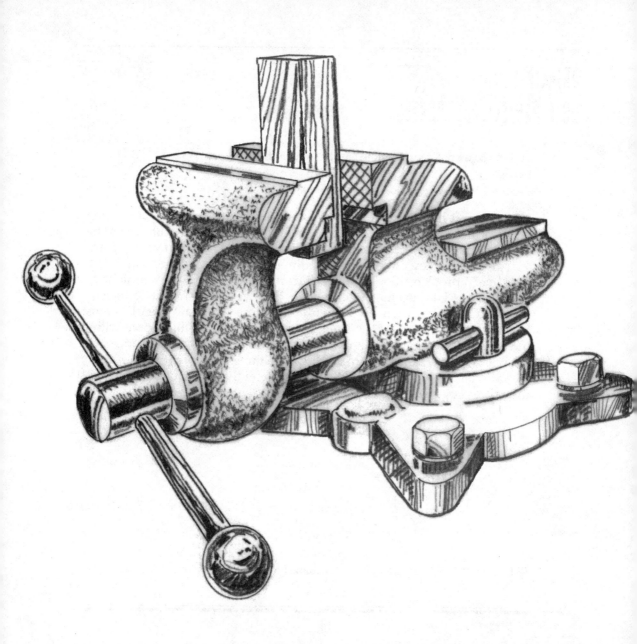

8 PRODUCT ASSURANCE PRINCIPLES

Product assurance is the set of activities that ensures the quality of software through the use of checks and balances. Product assurance generally includes:

1. *Software configuration management,* the process of managing changes to software.
2. *Software quality assurance,* the process of checking that all practices and products conform to established procedures and standards.
3. *Software verification and validation,* the processes of verifying that each intermediate product correctly builds upon the previous intermediate product and validating that each intermediate product satisfies the customer's requirements appropriately.
4. *Testing,* covered in an earlier chapter.

PRINCIPLE 173
PRODUCT ASSURANCE IS NOT A LUXURY

Product assurance includes software configuration management, software quality assurance, verification and validation, and testing. Of the four, the one whose necessity is most often acknowledged (though underbudgeted) is testing and evaluation. The other three are quite often dismissed as luxuries, as aspects of only large or expensive projects. The checks and balances these disciplines provide result in a significantly higher probability of producing a product that satisfies customer expectations and that is completed closer to schedule and cost goals. The key is to tailor the product assurance disciplines to the project in size, form, and content.

Ref: Siegel, S., "Why We Need Checks and Balances to Assure Quality," Quality Time Column, *IEEE Software, 9,* 1 (January 1992), pp. 102-103.

PRINCIPLE 174
ESTABLISH SCM PROCEDURES EARLY

Effective software configuration management (SCM) is not just having a tool that records who made what change to the code or documentation and when. It is also the thoughtful creation of naming conventions, policies, and procedures to ensure that all relevant parties are involved in changes to the software. It must be tailored to each project. Its presence means that:

- We know how to report a software problem.
- We know how to request a new requirement.
- All stakeholders are informed of suggested changes and their opinions are solicited.
- A board prioritizes and schedules change requests.
- All baselined intermediate or final products are under control (that is, it is impossible for them to be changed without following appropriate procedures).

The best place to record all of this is in a document, typically called the *software configuration management plan* (*SCMP*). This document should be written early in a project, typically getting approved around the same time the software requirements specification is approved.

Ref: Bersoff, E., V. Henderson, and S. Siegel, *Software Configuration Management*, Englewood Cliffs, N.J.: Prentice Hall, 1980, Section 5.4.

PRINCIPLE 175
ADAPT SCM TO SOFTWARE PROCESS

Software configuration management (SCM) is not a set of standard practices that apply uniformly to all projects. SCM must be tailored to each project's characteristics: size of the project, volatility, development process, extent of customer involvement, and so on. One size does not fit all.

For example, the U.S. Federal Aviation Administration's (FAA) National Airspace System (NAS) has a seven-level configuration control board; obviously that would be inappropriate for a small project. A throwaway prototype development could probably survive without a software requirements specification under configuration control; obviously a full-scale development project could not.

Ref: Bersoff, E., and A. Davis, "Impacts of Life Cycle Models on Software Configuration Management," *Communications of the ACM, 34,* 8 (August 1991), pp. 104-117.

PRINCIPLE 176
ORGANIZE SCM TO BE INDEPENDENT OF PROJECT MANAGEMENT

Software configuration management (SCM) can do its job properly only if it is independent of project management. Often, due to schedule pressure, a project manager may be tempted to bypass the very controls that enable a project to thrive in the long term. For example, in times of such schedule problems, the temptation might be to accept a new version of the software as a baseline even though no record was kept of which change requests were satisfied by it. If SCM reports to the project manager, there is little they can do but accept it. If they are independent, then SCM can enforce the rules that are best for everybody involved.

Ref: Bersoff, E., "Elements of Software Configuration Management," *IEEE Transactions on Software Engineering, 10,* 1 (January 1984), pp. 79-87.

PRINCIPLE 177
ROTATE PEOPLE THROUGH PRODUCT ASSURANCE

In many organizations, people are moved into product assurance organizations (1) as a first assignment or (2) after they have demonstrated poor performance at engineering software. Product assurance, however, requires the same level of engineering quality and discipline as designing and coding. As an alternative, rotate the best engineering talent through the product assurance organization. A good guideline might be that every excellent engineer spends six months in product assurance every two to three years. The expectation of all such engineers is that they will make significant improvements to product assurance during their "visit." Such a policy must clearly state that the job rotation is a reward for excellent performance.

Ref: Mendis, K., "Personnel Requirements to Make Software Quality Assurance Work," in *Handbook of Software Quality Assurance*, C.G. Schulmeyer, and J. McManus, eds., New York: Van Nostrand Reinhold, 1987, pp. 104-118.

PRINCIPLE 178
GIVE ALL INTERMEDIATE PRODUCTS A NAME AND VERSION

There is a multitude of intermediate products of software development: requirements specifications, design specifications, code, test plans, management plans, user's manuals, and so on. Every such product should be given a unique name, version/revision number, and date of creation. If any of them contain parts that can evolve relatively independently (such as, the software components in the program or the individual test plans in the overall test planning document), these parts should also be given unique names, version/revision numbers, and dates. "Parts lists" should enumerate all the parts that go with each version/revision of the intermediate product so that you know which versions and revisions of which parts comprise a specific version and revision of each intermediate product.

Furthermore, as a final product is released to a customer, it must be assigned a unique version/revision number (of the product) and dated. A release "parts list" then enumerates all the intermediate products (along with their respective version and release numbers) that comprise the product.

It is only with such naming that you can control the inevitable changes to a product (Principles 16 and 185).

Ref: Bersoff, E., V. Henderson, and S. Siegel, *Software Configuration Management,* Englewood Cliffs, N.J.: Prentice Hall, 1980, Chapter 4.

PRINCIPLE 179
CONTROL BASELINES

It is the responsibility of software configuration management to hold the agreed-upon specifications and regulate changes to them.

While repairing or enhancing a software component, a software engineer will occasionally discover something else that can be changed, perhaps to fix a yet unreported bug or to add some quick new feature. This kind of uncontrolled change is intolerable. See related Principle 187. SCM should avoid incorporating such changes into the new baseline. The correct procedure is for the software engineer to make a change request. This CR is then processed along with the others from development, marketing, testing, and the customers by a configuration control board, which prioritizes and schedules the change requests. Only then can the engineer be allowed to make the change and only then can SCM accept the change.

Ref: Bersoff, E., V. Henderson, and S. Siegel, *Software Configuration Management*, Englewood Cliffs, N.J.: Prentice Hall, 1980, Section 4.1.

PRINCIPLE 180
SAVE EVERYTHING

Paul Erlich has said, "The first rule of intelligent tinkering is to save all the parts." Software by its very nature is constantly being tinkered with. Since tinkering causes many errors (Principle 195), it is highly likely that any software change will need to be undone. The only way to do this is to ensure that everything is saved before a change is made. It is the software configuration management organization's job to save all copies of everything before an approved change is made to a baseline.

Ref: Erlich, P., as reported by Render, H., private communication, Colorado Springs, Col.: 1993.

PRINCIPLE 181
KEEP TRACK OF EVERY CHANGE

Every change has the potential to cause problems. Three common problems are:

1. The change did not fix the problem for which it was intended.
2. The change fixed the problem but caused others.
3. At a future date, the change is noticed and nobody can figure out why it was made (or by whom).

In all three cases the prevention is to track every change.

Tracking entails recording:

- The original request for change (this might be a customer's request for a new feature, a customer's complaint about a malfunction, a developer's detection of a problem, or a developer's desire to add a new feature).
- The approval process used to approve the change (who, when, why, in what release).
- The changes to all intermediate products (who, what, when).
- Appropriate cross-references among the change request, change approval, and changes themselves.

Such an audit trail enables you to easily back out, redo, and/or understand changes.

Ref: Bersoff, E., V. Henderson, and S. Siegel, *Software Configuration Management*, Englewood Cliffs, N.J.: Prentice Hall, 1980, Section 7.1.

PRINCIPLE 182
DON'T BYPASS CHANGE CONTROL

Everybody wins when changes are controlled. ("Controlled" does not mean "prevented.") Customers who have direct access to developers often bypass change control by asking individual developers to make specific changes for them. This is disastrous. It keeps project management in the dark. It causes costs to escalate. It renders the requirements specification inaccurate. How much worse could it get?

Ref: Curtis, B., H. Krasner, and N. Iscoe, "A Field Study of the Software Design Process for Large Systems," *Communications of the ACM, 31*, 11 (November 1988), pp. 1268-1287.

PRINCIPLE 183
RANK AND SCHEDULE CHANGE REQUESTS

On any product being used, change requests will funnel into the development organization from users, developers, and marketing personnel. These change requests may reflect desires for new features, reports of slow performance, or complaints about system errors. A committee should be formed, typically called a *configuration control board* (*CCB*), to regularly review all change requests. Their responsibility is to prioritize all of them and schedule when (or at least determine in which forthcoming release) they will be accommodated.

Ref: Whitgift, D., *Methods and Tools for Software Configuration Management*, New York: John Wiley & Sons, 1991, Chapter 9.

PRINCIPLE 184
USE VALIDATION AND VERIFICATION (V&V) ON
LARGE DEVELOPMENTS

Large software system developments need as many checks and balances as possible to ensure a quality product. One proven technique is the use of an organization independent of the development team to conduct validation and verification (V&V). *Validation* is the process of examining each intermediate product of software development to ensure that it conforms to the previous product. For example, validation ensures that software requirements meet system requirements, that high-level software design satisfies all the software requirements (and none other), that algorithms satisfy the component's external specification, that code implements the algorithms, and so on. *Verification* is the process of examining each intermediate product of software development to ensure that it satisfies the requirements.

You can think of V&V as a solution to the children's game of telephone. In telephone, a group of children form a chain and a specific oral message is whispered down the line. At the end, the last child tells what he/she heard, and it is rarely the same as the initial message. Validation would cause each child to ask the previous child, "Did you say x?" Verification would cause each child to ask the first child, "Did you say x?"

On a project, V&V should be planned early. It can be documented in the quality assurance plan or it can exist in a separate V&V plan. In either case, its procedures, players, actions, and results should be approved at roughly the same time the software requirements specification is approved.

Ref: Wallace, D., and R. Fujii, "Software Verification and Validation: An Overview," *IEEE Software*, 6, 3 (May 1989), pp. 10-17.

9 EVOLUTION PRINCIPLES

Evolution is the set of activities dealing with modifying the software product to:

1. Meet new functions.
2. Work more effectively.
3. Work correctly (when errors in the original product are detected).

PRINCIPLE 185
SOFTWARE WILL CONTINUE TO CHANGE

Any large software system that is being used will undergo continual change because the system's use will suggest additional functionality. It will change until it becomes more cost-effective to rewrite it from scratch. This is Manny Lehman's "Law of Continuing Change."

Ref: Lehman, M., "Programs, Cities, and Students—Limits to Growth?" Inaugural Lecture, Imperial College of Science and Technology, London (May 14, 1974); also see Belady, L., and M. Lehman, "A Model of Large Program Development," *IBM Systems Journal, 15,* 3 (March 1976), pp. 225-252.

PRINCIPLE 186
SOFTWARE'S ENTROPY INCREASES

Any software system that undergoes continuous change will grow in complexity and will become more and more disorganized. Since all software systems being used will change (Principle 185) and change causes instability, all useful software systems will migrate toward lower reliability and maintainability. This is Manny Lehman's "Law of Increasing Entropy."

Ref: Lehman, M., "Programs, Cities, and Students—Limits to Growth?" Inaugural Lecture, Imperial College of Science and Technology, London (May 14, 1974); also see Lehman, M., "Laws of Program Evolution—Rules and Tools for Programming Management," *InfoTech State of the Art Conference on Why Software Projects Fail* (April 1978), paper #11.

PRINCIPLE 187
IF IT AIN'T BROKE, DON'T FIX IT

Of course, this advice is applicable to many aspects of life, but it is particularly applicable to software. By its very name, software is considered malleable, easily modified. Don't be fooled into thinking that it is either easy to see or repair a "break" in software.

Suppose you are maintaining a system. You are examining the source code of a component. You are either trying to enhance it or seeking the cause of an error. While examining it, you detect what you believe is another error. Do not try to "repair" it. The probability is very high that you will introduce an error, not fix one (Principle 190). Instead, file a change request. Hopefully, the configuration control and associated technical reviews will determine if it is an error and what priority its repair should be given (Principles 175, 177, 178, and 179).

Ref: Reagan, R., as reported by Bentley, J., *More Programming Pearls*, Reading, Mass.: Addison-Wesley, 1988, Section 6.3.

PRINCIPLE 188
FIX PROBLEMS, NOT SYMPTOMS

When software fails, you have an obligation to fully understand the *cause* of the failure, not just to do a cursory analysis and apply a quick fix to what you *think* is the cause.

Suppose you are trying to trace the cause of a software failure. You have noticed that every time a specific component transmits a value, it is exactly twice the desired value. A quick and dirty solution is to divide the generated value by two just before it is transmitted. This solution is inappropriate because (1) it may not work for all cases, and (2) it leaves the program with what is essentially two errors that compensate for each other, rendering the program virtually unmaintainable in the future (Principle 92). An even worse quick and dirty solution is for the recipient to divide the value it receives by two before using it. This solution has all these problems associated with the first one, plus it causes all future components that invoke the faulty component to receive the wrong value. The *correct* solution is to examine the program and determine why the value is consistently doubled; *then* fix it.

Ref: McConnell, S., *Code Complete*, Redmond, Wash.: Microsoft Press, 1993, p. 638.

PRINCIPLE 189
CHANGE REQUIREMENTS FIRST

If all parties agree that an enhancement is to be made to the software, the first thing to do is to update the software requirements specification and get it approved. Only after this is done is there a high probability that customers, marketing personnel, and developers will really agree to what the change is. Sometimes time restrictions make it impossible to do this (and this should not be all the time, or management needs to read the management principles in this book!). In that case, initiate changes to the SRS before starting changes to the design and code, and approve the changes to the SRS before finishing changes to the design and code.

Ref: Arthur, J., *Software Evolution*, New York: John Wiley & Sons, 1988, Chapter 6.

PRINCIPLE 190
PRERELEASE ERRORS YIELD POSTRELEASE ERRORS

Components with high rates of prerelease errors will also have high rates of postrelease errors. This is disappointing news for developers, but fully supported by empirical data (and by Principle 114, which implies that, the more errors you find in a component, the more you will still find). The best advice is to discard, replace, and recreate from scratch any component with a poor history. Don't throw good money after bad.

Ref: Dunn, R., *Software Defect Removal*, New York: McGraw-Hill, 1984, Section 10.2.

PRINCIPLE 191
THE OLDER A PROGRAM, THE MORE DIFFICULT IT IS TO MAINTAIN

As a change is made to a software system (whether for repair or enhancement), a certain number of components of that system must be altered. As a program gets older, the percentage of total system components that must be altered for each change grows. Every change makes all subsequent changes more difficult because the program's structure necessarily deteriorates.

Ref: Belady, L., and B. Leavenworth, "Program Modifiability," in *Software Engineering,* Freeman, H., and P. Lewis, eds., New York: Academic Press, 1980, pp. 26-27.

PRINCIPLE 192
LANGUAGE AFFECTS MAINTAINABILITY

The programming language used for development significantly affects productivity during maintenance. Certain languages, such as APL, Basic, and LISP, facilitate the rapid development of functions, but they are inherently difficult to maintain. Other languages, such as Ada or Pascal, offer challenges in development but are inherently easier to maintain. Languages that tend to force high cohesion and low coupling (Principle 73), such as Eiffel, usually facilitate both development and subsequent maintenance. Languages at very low levels, like assembler, usually inhibit productivity during both development and maintenance. Contrast this with Principle 99.

Ref: Boehm, B., *Software Engineering Economics*, Englewood Cliffs, N.J.: Prentice Hall, 1981, Section 30.4.

PRINCIPLE 193
SOMETIMES IT IS BETTER TO START OVER

There is so much talk these days about reengineering, renovation, and reverse engineering that we may all start believing it is easy to do. It is hard to do. Sometimes it makes much sense; it is worth the investment. Other times it is a waste of scarce resources, and it would be better to just design and code from scratch. Ask yourselves, for example, will the maintainers really use design documentation if you produce it?

Ref: Agresti, W., "Low-Tech Tips for High Quality Software," Quality Time Column, *IEEE Software*, 9, 6 (November 1991), pp. 86, 87-89.

PRINCIPLE 194
RENOVATE THE WORST FIRST

Principle 193 suggests that starting over may sometimes be the best idea. Another less painful approach is to completely redesign and recode the worst components. Here "worst" means those that consume the most corrective maintenance dollars. Gerald Weinberg reports that on one system rewriting one 800-line module (that consumed 30 percent of all corrective maintenance costs) saved considerable resources on the entire maintenance effort.

Ref: Weinberg, G., "Software Maintenance," *Datalink* (May 14, 1979), as reported by Arthur, J., *Software Evolution*, New York: John Wiley & Sons, 1988, Chapter 12.

PRINCIPLE 195
MAINTENANCE CAUSES MORE ERRORS THAN DEVELOPMENT

Fixes to a program during maintenance (whether enhancement or defect correction) introduce far more errors than initial development. Maintenance organizations report that between 20 and 50 percent of all changes made during maintenance introduce more errors.

It is for this reason that conformity to "the rules" is so important: Establish an SCM plan (Principle 174), control baselines (Principle 179), and don't bypass change control (Principle 182).

Ref: Humphrey, W., "Quality From Both Developer and User Viewpoints," Quality Time Column, *IEEE Software*, 6, 5 (September 1989), pp. 84, 100.

PRINCIPLE 196
REGRESSION TEST AFTER EVERY CHANGE

Regression testing is the testing of all previously tested features after a change is made. Most people bypass regression testing because they think their change is innocent.

You have just made a change to a module either to repair an error (corrective maintenance), to add a new feature (adaptive maintenance), or to increase its performance (perfective maintenance). You must test that what you did worked correctly. That is, you have to try out that which worked improperly before, see if the new feature works, or verify that performance is improved. If the test passes, are you done? Absolutely not! Software unfortunately does strange things. You must also do regression testing to verify that everything that worked correctly before still works.

Ref: McConnell, S., *Code Complete*, Redmond, Wash.: Microsoft Press, 1993, Section 25.6.

PRINCIPLE 197
BELIEF THAT A CHANGE IS EASY MAKES IT LIKELY IT WILL BE MADE INCORRECTLY

This is Gerald Weinberg's "Self-Invalidating Model" principle and relates strongly to the more generic situation described in Principle 171. Since software is complex and its correct behavior depends upon "perfection," the implications of every change to it must be considered seriously. As soon as developers think a change is simple, easy, or self-evident, their guard is down, quality instilling approaches are disregarded, and in most cases the change is made incorrectly. This is manifest either as an incorrect change or as an unintended side-effect.

To prevent this situation, be sure the change you are doing is approved (Principles 182 and 183), desk-check every change (Principle 97), and regression test after every set of changes (Principle 196).

Ref: Weinberg, G., *Quality Software Management*, Vol. 1: Systems Thinking, New York: Dorset House, 1992, Section 15.2.3.

PRINCIPLE 198
STRUCTURING UNSTRUCTURED CODE DOES NOT NECESSARILY IMPROVE IT

Let's say you have to maintain a program that was written in an unstructured manner. You could mechanically transform the code into an equivalent one that is structured and that still performs the same function. Such a program is not necessarily better! Often such mechanical restructuring results in equally poor code. Instead, rethink the module and redesign it from scratch, using sound software engineering principles.

Ref: Arthur, J., *Software Evolution*, New York: John Wiley & Sons, 1988, Sections 7.2 and 9.1.

PRINCIPLE 199
USE PROFILER BEFORE OPTIMIZING

When it is time to optimize a program to make it faster, remember that 80 percent of the CPU cycles will be consumed by 20 percent of the code (Pareto). Therefore, first find the 20 percent of the code whose optimization will yield results. The best way to do this is to use any commercially available profiler. A *profiler* monitors your program while it is executing and identifies the "hot spots," that is, sections that consume the most CPU cycles. Optimize these.

Ref: Morton, M., as reported by Bentley, J., *More Programming Pearls*, Reading, Mass.: Addison-Wesley, 1988, Section 6.4.

PRINCIPLE 200
CONSERVE FAMILIARITY

This is Manny Lehman's "Law of Conservation of Familiarity." As a software product is maintained, incremental releases are made. Each new release contains some amount of growth (that is, divergence from the familiar behavior of earlier releases). Releases that display larger-than-average new growth will tend to have "poor performance, poor reliability, high fault rates, and cost and time overruns." Furthermore, the greater the growth from the average, the higher the risk. The reason for this phenomenon appears to be the stabilization effect of releasing software to users. Since software change tends to cause instability (Principles 184 and 190), a large number of changes between releases can cause a degree of instability that cannot be compensated for by a release. In addition, the amount of psychological familiarity that developers feel for a product decreases during the time between releases; that is, the longer the software is modified, the stranger it "feels" to the developers. Upon product release, a major relearning process occurs and developers once again feel comfortable. If too many changes are made between releases, too many changes get made to "unfamiliar" code and quality suffers.

Bottom line: Be relatively consistent with the amount of changes made between product releases.

Ref: Lehman, M., "On Understanding Laws, Evolution, and Conservation in the Large-Program Life Cycle," *Journal of Systems and Software, 1,* 3 (September 1980), pp. 213-221.

PRINCIPLE 201
THE SYSTEM'S EXISTENCE PROMOTES EVOLUTION

Let's assume for a moment that we could do a "perfect" job of requirements specification up front. Let's further assume for a moment that requirements didn't change during development, so that when the system is created it actually satisfies the needs that exist. Even if these assumptions were valid, evolution would still go on because the insertion of the system in its problem environment changes that environment and thus causes new problems.

What this means is that, no matter how good a handle you think you have on the requirements, you must plan for the changes that will be necessary after deployment.

Ref: Lehman, M., "Software Engineering, the Software Process, and Their Support," *Software Engineering Journal, 6,* 5 (September 1991), pp. 243-258.

REFERENCES INDEX

Abdel-Hamid, T., and S. Madnick, "Impact on Schedule Estimation on Software Project Behavior," *IEEE Software*, 3, 4 (July 1986), pp. 70-75. *(Principle 156)*

Agresti, W., "Low-Tech Tips for High Quality Software," Quality Time Column, *IEEE Software*, 9, 6 (November 1991), pp. 86, 87-89. *(Principle 193)*

Alexander, L., and A. Davis, "Criteria for the Selection of a Software Process Model," *IEEE COMPSAC '91*, Washington, D.C.: IEEE Computer Society Press, pp. 521-528. *(Principle 163)*

Andriole, S., "Storyboard Prototyping for Requirements Verification," *Large Scale Systems*, 12 (1987), pp. 231-247. *(Principle 42)*

Andriole, S., *Rapid Application Prototyping*, Wellesley, Mass.: QED, 1992. *(Principle 13)*

Arthur, J., *Software Evolution*, New York: John Wiley & Sons, 1988, Chapter 6; Sections 7.2, 9.1. *(Principles 189, 198)*

Basili, V., and J. Musa, "The Future Engineering of Software: A Management Perspective," *IEEE Computer*, 24, 9 (September 1991), pp. 90-96. *(Principle 36)*

Belady, L., and B. Leavenworth, "Program Modifiability," in *Software Engineering*, Freeman, H., and P. Lewis, eds., New York: Academic Press, 1980, pp. 26-27. *(Principle 191)*

Belady, L., and M. Lehman, "A Model of Large Program Development," *IBM Systems Journal*, 15, 3 (March 1976), pp. 225-252. *(Principle 185)*

Bennis, W., *The Unconscious Conspiracy: Why Leaders Can't Lead*, New York: AMACOM, 1976. *(Principle 135)*

Bersoff, E., "Elements of Software Configuration Management," *IEEE Transactions on Software Engineering*, 10, 1 (January 1984), pp. 79-87. *(Principle 176)*

Bersoff, E., and A. Davis, "Impacts of Life Cycle Models on Software Configuration Management," *Communications of the ACM, 34,* 8 (August 1991), pp. 104-117. *(Principle 175)*

Bersoff, E., V. Henderson, and S. Siegel, *Software Configuration Management,* Englewood Cliffs, N.J.: Prentice Hall, 1980, Chapter 4, Sections 2.2, 4.1, 5.4, 7.1. *(Principles 16, 174, 178, 179, 181)*

Berzins, V., and Luqi, *Software Engineering with Abstractions,* Reading, Mass.: Addison-Wesley, 1991, Section 1.5. *(Principle 106)*

Boehm, B., "The High Cost of Software," in *Practical Strategies for Developing Large Software Systems,* E. Horowitz, ed., Reading, Mass.: Addison-Wesley, 1975. *(Principle 168)*

Boehm, B., "Software Engineering," *IEEE Transactions on Computers, 25,* 12 (December 1976), pp. 1226-1241. *(Principle 41)*

Boehm, B., *Software Engineering Economics,* Englewood Cliffs, N.J.: Prentice Hall, 1981, Sections 26.5, 27.3, 29.9, 30.4, 32.7, 33.4. *(Principles 104, 146, 148, 150, 152, 192)*

Boehm, B., "Seven Basic Principles of Software Engineering," *Journal of Systems and Software, 3,* 1 (March 1983), pp. 3-24. *(Preface)*

Boehm, B., "Verifying and Validating Software Requirements and Design Specifications," *IEEE Software, 1,* 1 (January 1984), pp. 75-88. *(Principles 40, 45)*

Boehm, B., "Software Risk Management: Principles and Practices," *IEEE Software, 9,* 1 (January 1991), pp. 32-39. *(Principle 161)*

Brooks, F., *The Mythical Man-Month,* Reading, Mass.: Addison-Wesley, 1975, Chapters 2, 4. *(Principles 140, 160)*

Brooks, F., "No Silver Bullet: Essence and Accidents of Software Engineering," *IEEE Computer, 20,* 4 (April 1987), pp. 10-19. *(Principles 17, 72, 82)*

Charette, R., *Software Engineering Risk Analysis and Management,* New York: McGraw-Hill, 1989, Section 2.2, Chapter 6. *(Principles 162)*

Cherry, G., *Software Construction by Object-Oriented Pictures,* Canadaigua, New York: Thought Tools, 1990, p. 39. *(Principle 61)*

Chikofsky, E., "Changing Your Endgame Strategy," *IEEE Software, 7,* 6 (November 1990), pp. 87, 112. *(Principle 172)*

Constantine, L., and E. Yourdon, *Structured Design,* Englewood Cliffs, N.J.: Prentice Hall, 1979. *(Principle 73)*

Curtis, B., H. Krasner, and N. Iscoe, "A Field Study of the Software Design Process for Large Systems," *Communications of the ACM, 31,* 11 (November 1988), pp. 1268-1287. *(Principles 15, 83, 136, 182)*

Davis A., "A Comparison of Techniques for the Specification of External System Behavior," *Communications of the ACM, 31,* 9 (September 1988), pp. 1098-1115. *(Principle 47)*

Davis, A., "Operational Prototyping: A New Development Approach," *IEEE Software, 9,* 5 (September 1992), pp. 70-78. *(Principles 11, 12)*

Davis, A., *Software Requirements: Objects, Functions and States,* Englewood Cliffs, N.J.: Prentice Hall, 1993, Sections 3.1, 3.4.2, 3.4.6, 3.4.11, 5.3.2. *(Principles 46, 49, 50, 53, 56, 58)*

Davis, A., "Software Lemmingineering," *IEEE Software, 10,* 6 (September 1993), pp. 79-81, 84. *(Principle 30)*

Davis, A., and E. Comer, "No Crystal Ball in the Software Industry," *IEEE Software, 10,* 4 (July 1993), pp. 91-94, 97. *(Principles 169, 170)*

DeMarco, T., "Why Does Software Cost So Much?" *IEEE Software, 10,* 2 (March 1993), pp. 89-90. *(Principles 147, 157)*

DeMarco, T., and T. Lister, *Peopleware,* New York: Dorset House, 1987, Chapters 6, 12. *(Principles 139, 165)*

Dijkstra, E., "Notes on Structured Programming," in *Structured Programming,* Dahl, O., et al., eds., New York: Academic Press, 1972. *(Principle 111)*

Dunn, R., *Software Defect Removal,* New York: McGraw-Hill, 1984, Sections 7.2, 7.4, 10.2, 10.3. *(Principles 115, 121, 123, 190)*

Endres, A., "An Analysis of Errors and Their Causes in System Programs," *IEEE Transactions on Software Engineering, 1,* 2 (June 1975), pp. 140-149. *(Principle 114)*

Erlich, P., as reported by Render, H., private communication, Colorado Springs, Col.: 1993. *(Principle 180)*

Fairley, R., *Software Engineering Concepts,* New York: McGraw-Hill, 1985. *(Principle 69)*

Fairley, R., "Recent Advances in Software Estimation Techniques," *14th IEEE International Conference on Software Engineering,* Washington, D.C.: IEEE Computer Society Press, 1992. *(Principle 145)*

Farbman, D., "Myths That Miss," *Datamation* (November 1980), pp. 109-112. *(Principle 8)*

Fenton, N., "How Effective Are Software Engineering Methods?" *Journal of Systems and Software*, 22, 2 (August 1993), pp. 141-146. *(Principles 127, 129)*

Floyd, C., "A Systematic Look at Prototyping," in *Approaches to Prototyping*, R. Budde, et al., Berlin, Germany: Springer Verlag, 1983, pp. 1-18, Section 3.1. *(Principle 5)*

Francis, P., *Principles of R&D Management*, New York: AMACOM, 1977, pp. 114-116. *(Principle 133)*

Gause, D., and G. Weinberg, *Are Your Lights On?* New York: Dorset House, 1990. *(Principle 39)*

Gerhart, S., and L. Yelowitz, "Observations of Fallibility in Applications of Modern Programming Methodologies," *IEEE Transactions on Software Engineering*, 2, 3 (September 1976), pp. 195-207, Section I. *(Principle 126)*

Gilb, T., "Deadline Pressure: How to Cope with Short Deadlines, Low Budgets and Insufficient Staffing Levels," in *Information Processing*, H.J. Kugler, ed., Amsterdam: Elsevier Publishers, 1986. *(Principle 130)*

Gilb, T., *Principles of Software Engineering Management*, Reading, Mass.: Addison-Wesley, 1988, Sections 7.14, 8.10, 9.11, 16.7. *(Principles 43, 52, 154, 155)*

Glaser, G., "Managing Projects in the Computer Industry," *IEEE Computer*, 17, 10 (October 1984), pp. 45-53. *(Principle 158)*

Glass, R., *Building Quality Software*, Englewood Cliffs, N.J.: Prentice Hall, 1992, Section 2.2.2.5. *(Principle 62)*

Gomaa, H., and D. Scott, "Prototyping as a Tool in the Specification of User Requirements," *Fifth International Conference on Software Engineering*, Washington, D.C.: IEEE Computer Society Press, 1981, pp. 333-342. *(Principle 7)*

Goodenough, J., and S. Gerhart, "Toward a Theory of Test Data Selection," *IEEE Transactions on Software Engineering*, 1, 2 (June 1975), pp. 156-173, Section IIIC. *(Principles 108, 113)*

Grady, R., and T. VanSlack, "Key Lessons in Achieving Widespread Inspection Use," *IEEE Software*, 11, 4 (July 1994), pp. 46-57. *(Principle 98)*

Hall, A., "Seven Myths of Formal Methods," *IEEE Software*, 7, 5 (September 1990), pp. 11-19. *(Principle 28)*

Herzberg, F., "One More Time: How Do You Motivate Employees?" *Harvard Business Review* (September-October 1987). *(Principle 138)*

Hoare, C.A.R., "Software Engineering: A Keynote Address," *IEEE 3rd International Conference on Software Engineering*, 1978, pp. 1-4. *(Principle 37)*

Hoare, C.A.R., "Programming: Sorcery or Science?" *IEEE Software, 1,* 2 (April 1984), pp. 14-15. *(Principle 18)*

Horowitz, E., and S. Sahni, *Fundamentals of Computer Algorithms*, Potomac, Md.: Computer Science Press, 1978. *(Principle 79)*

Huang, J., "Program Instrumentation and Software Testing," *IEEE Computer, 11,* 4 (April 1978), pp. 25-32. *(Principle 124)*

Huff, C., "Elements of a Realistic CASE Tool Adoption Budget," *Communications of the ACM, 35,* 4 (April 1992), pp. 45-54. *(Principle 25)*

Humphrey, W., "Quality From Both Developer and User Viewpoints," Quality Time Column, *IEEE Software, 6,* 5 (September 1989), pp. 84, 100. *(Principle 195)*

IEEE Computer Society, *Software Engineering Standards Collection*, Washington, D.C.: IEEE Computer Society Press, 1993. *(Principle 32)*

IEEE, *ANSI/IEEE Guide to Software Requirements Specifications*, Standard 830-1994, Washington, D.C.: IEEE Computer Society Press, 1994. *(Principle 59)*

Incorvaia, A. J., A. Davis, and R. Fairley, "Case Studies in Software Reuse," *Fourteenth IEEE International Conference on Computer Software and Applications*, Washington, D.C.: IEEE Computer Society Press, 1990, pp. 301-306. *(Principle 84)*

Jones, C., *Programming Productivity*, New York: McGraw-Hill, 1986, Chapter 1. *(Principle 144)*

Joyce, E., "Is Error-Free Software Achievable?" *Datamation* (February 15, 1989). *(Principle 4)*

Kajihara, J., G. Amamiya, and T. Saya, "Learning from Bugs," *IEEE Software, 10,* 5 (September 1993), pp. 46-54. *(Principle 125)*

Kemerer, C., "How the Learning Curve Affects Tool Adoption," *IEEE Software, 9,* 3 (May 1992), pp. 23-28. *(Principles 22, 23)*

Kernighan, B., and P. Plauger, *The Elements of Programming Style*, New York: McGraw-Hill, 1978, pp. 20-37, 52, 67, 124-134, 141-144. *(Principles 89, 93-95)*

Lederer, A., and J. Prasad, "Nine Management Guidelines for Better Cost Estimating," *Communications of the ACM, 35,* 2 (February 1992), pp. 51-59, Guideline 1. *(Principles 38, 153)*

Ledgard, H., *Programming Proverbs,* Rochelle Park, N.J.: Hayden Book Company, 1975, Proverbs 8, 21; pp. 94-98. *(Principles 90, 91, 97)*

Ledgard, H., *Programming Practice,* Vol. II, Reading, Mass.: Addison-Wesley, 1987, Chap. 4. *(Principle 88)*

Lehman, M., "Programs, Cities, and Students—Limits to Growth?" Inaugural Lecture, Imperial College of Science and Technology, London (May 14, 1974). *(Principles 185, 186)*

Lehman, M., "Laws of Program Evolution—Rules and Tools for Programming Management," *InfoTech State of the Art Conference on Why Software Projects Fail* (April 1978), paper #11. *(Principle 186)*

Lehman, M., "On Understanding Laws, Evolution, and Conservation in the Large-Program Life Cycle," *Journal of Systems and Software, 1,* 3 (July 1980), pp. 213-221. *(Preface)*

Lehman, M., "On Understanding Laws, Evolution, and Conservation in the Large-Program Life Cycle," *Journal of Systems and Software, 1,* 3 (September 1980), pp. 213-221. *(Principle 200)*

Lehman, M., "Programming Productivity—A Life Cycle Concept," *COMPCON 81,* Washington, D.C.: IEEE Computer Society Press, 1981, Section 1.1. *(Principle 3)*

Lehman, M., "Software Engineering, the Software Process and Their Support," *Software Engineering Journal, 6,* 5 (September 1991), pp. 243-258, Section 3.6. *(Principles 20, 201)*

Lehman, M., private communication, Colorado Springs, Col.: (January 24, 1994). *(Principle 110)*

Lehman, M., private communication, Colorado Springs, Col.: (January 25, 1994). *(Principle 151)*

Lindstrom, D., "Five Ways to Destroy a Development Project," *IEEE Software, 10,* 5 (September 1992), pp. 55-58. *(Principle 107)*

Loy, P., "The Method Won't Save You (But It Can Help)," *ACM Software Engineering Notes, 18,* 1 (January 1993), pp. 30-34. *(Principle 164)*

Macro, A., *Software Engineering: Concepts and Management,* Englewood Cliffs, N.J.: Prentice-Hall International, 1990, p. 247. *(Principle 87)*

Matsubara, T., "Bringing up Software Designers," *American Programmer, 3,* 7 (July-August 1990), pp. 15-18. *(Principle 21)*

McCabe, T., "A Complexity Measure," *IEEE Transactions on Software Engineering, 2,* 12 (December 1976), pp. 308-320. *(Principle 120)*

McConnell, S., *Code Complete,* Redmond, Wash.: Microsoft Press, 1993, Chapter 18; p. 638; Sections 3.5, 4.2-4.4, 5.6, 17.4, 17.6, 25.6, 32.3. *(Principles 85, 92, 96, 99, 101, 102, 105, 188, 196)*

McGregor, D., *The Human Side of Enterprise,* New York: McGraw-Hill, 1960. *(Principle 134)*

Mendis, K., "Personnel Requirements to Make Software Quality Assurance Work," in *Handbook of Software Quality Assurance,* C.G. Schulmeyer, and J. McManus, eds., New York: Van Nostrand Reinhold, 1987, pp. 104-118. *(Principle 177)*

Meyer, B., "On Formalism in Specifications," *IEEE Software, 2,* 1 (January 1985), pp. 6-26. *(Principles 35, 54)*

Miller, G., "The Magical Number Seven, Plus or Minus Two," *The Psychological Review, 63,* 2 (March 1956), pp. 81-97. *(Principle 67)*

Mills, H., "Top-Down Programming in Large Systems," in *Debugging Techniques in Large Systems,* R. Ruskin, ed., Englewood Cliffs, N.J.: Prentice Hall, 1971. *(Principle 14)*

Mizuno, Y., "Software Quality Improvement," *IEEE Computer, 16,* 3 (March 1983), pp. 66-72. *(Principle 29)*

Morton, M., as reported by Bentley, J., *More Programming Pearls,* Reading, Mass.: Addison-Wesley, 1988, Section 6.4. *(Principle 199)*

Musa, J., A. Iannino, and K. Okumoto, *Software Reliability,* New York: McGraw-Hill, 1987, Section 4.2.2. *(Principle 86)*

Myers, G., *The Art of Software Testing,* New York: John Wiley & Sons, 1979, pp. 12, 14, 113-114. *(Principles 109, 116-118)*

Parnas, D., "A Technique for Software Module Specification with Examples," *Communications of the ACM, 15,* 5 (May 1972), pp. 330-336. *(Principle 80)*

Parnas, D., "On the Criteria to Be Used in Decomposing Systems into Modules," *Communications of the ACM, 15,* 12 (December 1972), pp. 1053-1058. *(Principle 65)*

Parnas, D., "Designing Software for Ease of Extension and Contraction," *IEEE Transactions on Software Engineering, 5,* 2 (March 1979), pp. 128-138. *(Principles 44, 77, 78)*

Pfleeger, S., "Lessons Learned in Building a Corporate Metrics Program," *IEEE Software, 10,* 3 (May 1993), pp. 67-74. *(Principle 143)*

Ramamoorthy, C. V., V. Garg, and A. Prakash, "Programming in the Large," *IEEE Transactions on Software Engineering, 12*, 7 (July 1986), pp. 769-783. *(Principle 66)*

Rauscher, T., private communication, 1977. *(Principle 137)*

Reagan, R., as reported by Bentley, J., *More Programming Pearls*, Reading, Mass.: Addison-Wesley, 1988, Section 6.3. *(Principle 187)*

Reifer, D., "The Nature of Software Management: A Primer," *Tutorial: Software Management*, D. Reifer, ed., Washington, D.C.: IEEE Computer Society Press, 1986, pp. 42-45. *(Principles 132, 159)*

Romach, H. D., "Design Measurement: Some Lessons Learned," *IEEE Software, 7*, 2 (March 1990), pp. 17-25. *(Principle 75)*

Royce, W., "Managing the Development of Large Software Systems," *WESCON '70*, 1970; reprinted in *9th International Conference on Software Engineering*, Washington, D.C.: IEEE Computer Society Press, 1987, pp. 328-338. *(Preface, Principles 10, 64)*

Sackman, H., et al., "Exploratory Experimental Studies Comparing Online and Offline Programming Performance," *Communications of the ACM, 11*, 1 (January 1968), pp. 3-11. *(Principle 141)*

Siegel, S., "Why We Need Checks and Balances to Assure Quality," Quality Time Column, *IEEE Software, 9*, 1 (January 1992), pp. 102-103. *(Principle 173)*

Sommerville, I., *Software Engineering*, Reading, Mass.: Addison-Wesley, 1992, Sections 20.0, 20.1. *(Principles 6, 57)*

Stark, G., R. Durst, and C. Vowell, "Using Metrics in Management Decision-Making," *IEEE Computer, 27*, 9 (September 1994). *(Principle 149)*

Turski, W., oral comments made at a conference in the late 1970s. *(Principle 19)*

U.S. Air Force, *Cost/Schedule Management of Non-Major Contracts*, Air Force Systems Command Publication #178-3, Andrews AFB, Md.: (November 1978). *(Principle 166)*

Wallace, D., and R. Fujii, "Software Verification and Validation: An Overview," *IEEE Software, 6*, 3 (May 1989), pp. 10-17. *(Principle 184)*

Weinberg, G., *The Psychology of Computer Programming*, New York: Van Nostrand Reinhold, 1971, Chapters 6-7. *(Principle 131)*

Weinberg, G., "Software Maintenance," *Datalink* (May 14, 1979), as reported by Arthur, J., *Software Evolution*, New York: John Wiley & Sons, 1988, Chapter 12. *(Principle 194)*

Weinberg, G., *Rethinking Systems Analysis and Design*, New York: Dorset House, 1988, Part V. *(Principle 63)*

Weinberg, G., *Quality Software Management*, Vol. 1: Systems Thinking, New York: Dorset House, 1992, Sections 1.2, 12.1.2, 13.2.3, 15.2.3, 15.3.5. *(Principles 2, 112, 119, 171, 197)*

Weinberg, G., and E. Schulman, "Goals and Performance in Computer Programming," *Human Factors, 16* (1974), pp. 70-77. *(Principle 142)*

Weiser, M., J. Gannon, and P. McMullin, "Comparison of Structural Test Coverage Metrics," *IEEE Software, 2,* 2 (March 1985), pp. 80-85. *(Principle 122)*

Whitgift, D., *Methods and Tools for Software Configuration Management*, New York: John Wiley & Sons, 1991, Chapter 9. *(Principle 183)*

Witt, B., F. Baker, and E. Merritt, *Software Architecture and Design*, New York: Van Nostrand Reinhold, 1994, Sections 1.1, 1.3, 2.5, 2.6, 6.4.2.6. *(Principles 70, 71, 74, 76, 81)*

Yeh, R., P. Zave, A. Conn, and G. Cole, Jr., "Software Requirements: New Directions and Perspectives," in *Handbook of Software Engineering*, C. Vick and C. Ramamoorthy, eds., New York: Van Nostrand Reinhold, 1984, pp. 519-543. *(Principle 48)*

Yourdon, E., *How to Manage Structured Programming*, New York: Yourdon, Inc., 1976, Sections 5.2.2, 5.2.5. *(Principles 100, 103)*

Yourdon, E., *Decline and Fall of the American Programmer*, Englewood Cliffs, N.J.: Prentice Hall, 1992 (Chapter 8). *(Principle 1)*

Zerouni, C., as reported by Bentley, J., *More Programming Pearls*, Reading, Mass.: Addison-Wesley, 1988, Section 6.1. *(Principle 68)*

SUBJECT INDEX